TECHNICAL REPORT

Emergency Responder Injuries and Fatalities

An Analysis of Surveillance Data

ARI N. HOUSER, BRIAN A. JACKSON,
JAMES T. BARTIS, D. J. PETERSON

TR-100-NIOSH

March 2004

Prepared for the National Personal Protective Technology Laboratory

 SCIENCE AND TECHNOLOGY

The research described in this report was conducted by the Science and Technology Policy Institute (operated by RAND from 1992 to November 2003) for the National Personal Protective Technology Laboratory.

Library of Congress Cataloging-in-Publication Data

Emergency responder injuries and fatalities : an analysis of surveillance data / Ari N. Houser ... [et al.].
    p. cm.
    "TR-100."
    Includes bibliographical references.
    ISBN 0-8330-3565-7 (pbk.)
    1. Emergency medical personnel—Wounds and injuries. 2. Emergency medical personnel—Health and hygiene.
    [DNLM: 1. Accidents, Occupational. 2. Emergency Medicine. 3. Risk. 4. Wounds and Injuries. WA 487 E53 2004] I. Houser, Ari N. II. Rand Corporation.

RC965.E48E47 2004
614'.3'08836218—dc22

2004001260

The RAND Corporation is a nonprofit research organization providing objective analysis and effective solutions that address the challenges facing the public and private sectors around the world. RAND's publications do not necessarily reflect the opinions of its research clients and sponsors.

RAND® is a registered trademark.

Published 2004 by the RAND Corporation
1700 Main Street, P.O. Box 2138, Santa Monica, CA 90407-2138
1200 South Hayes Street, Arlington, VA 22202-5050
201 North Craig Street, Suite 202, Pittsburgh, PA 15213-1516
RAND URL: http://www.rand.org/
To order RAND documents or to obtain additional information, contact
Distribution Services: Telephone: (310) 451-7002;
Fax: (310) 451-6915; Email: order@rand.org

Preface

In FY 2001, the National Institute for Occupational Safety and Health (NIOSH) established the National Personal Protective Technology Laboratory (NPPTL). This new laboratory endeavors to reduce and prevent occupational disease, injury, and death of workers by advancing federal research on personal protective technologies. Technologies of interest to NPPTL include devices such as respirators, chemical-resistant clothing, hearing protection, and safety goggles and glasses that provide a barrier between the worker and an occupational safety or health risk. Other personal protective technologies include devices that provide a worker with early warning of a hazard or otherwise help keep the worker safe from harm, such as sensors that detect toxic atmospheres, and communication devices used for safe deployment of workers.

Because emergency responders face significant hazards as they carry out their missions, NPPTL selected this group of workers to be an early focus of its program. In the wake of September 11, 2001, when so many emergency responders were injured and killed responding to terrorist attacks at the World Trade Center and the Pentagon, the significance of this mission has become even more apparent.

NPPTL asked the RAND Science and Technology Policy Institute to review available databases that offer to provide disease, injury, and fatality data pertinent to emergency response functions and the role of personal protective technology.

Surveillance data resources exist that describe the injuries, illnesses, and fatalities suffered by emergency responders. These data sources, maintained by both responder community organizations and government agencies, contain valuable information concerning the hazards facing firefighters, police, and emergency medical responders. This technical report summarizes the results of an analysis of available surveillance data sources. That analysis, along with the interests and concerns of the emergency responder community and the expertise of NIOSH staff, will support development of potential objectives and related research tasks directed at providing personal protective technologies to emergency responders.

The Science and Technology Policy Institute

Originally created by Congress in 1991 as the Critical Technologies Institute and renamed in 1998, the Science and Technology Policy Institute is a federally funded research and development center sponsored by the National Science Foundation. The institute was managed by the RAND Corporation from 1992 through November 30, 2003.

The institute's mission is to help improve public policy by conducting objective, independent research and analysis on policy issues that involve science and technology. To this end, the institute

- supports the Office of Science and Technology Policy and other Executive Branch agencies, offices, and councils

- helps science and technology decisionmakers understand the likely consequences of their decisions and choose among alternative policies

- helps improve understanding in both the public and private sectors of the ways in which science and technology can better serve national objectives.

In carrying out its mission, the institute consults broadly with representatives from private industry, institutions of higher education, and other nonprofit institutions.

Inquiries regarding the Science and Technology Policy Institute may be directed to the addresses below.

Stephen Rattien
Director, RAND Science and Technology
1200 South Hayes Street
Arlington, VA 22202-5050
Phone: (703) 413-1100 x5219
http://www.rand.org/scitech/stpi/

The RAND Corporation Quality Assurance Process

Peer review is an integral part of all RAND research projects. Prior to publication, this document, as with all documents in the RAND technical report series, was subject to a quality assurance process to ensure that the research meets several standards, including the following: The problem is well formulated; the research approach is well designed and well executed; the data and assumptions are sound; the findings are useful and advance knowledge; the implications and recommendations follow logically from the findings and are explained thoroughly; the documentation is accurate, understandable, cogent, and temperate in tone; the research demonstrates understanding of related previous studies; and the research is relevant, objective, independent, and balanced. Peer review is conducted by research professionals who were not members of the project team.

RAND routinely reviews and refines its quality assurance process and also conducts periodic external and internal reviews of the quality of its body of work. For additional details regarding the RAND quality assurance process, visit http://www.rand.org/standards/.

Table of Contents

Figures

Tables

Acronyms

ATSDR	Agency for Toxic Substances and Disease Registry
BJS	Bureau of Justice Statistics
BLS	Bureau of Labor Statistics
CFOI	Census of Fatal Occupational Injuries
EMS	Emergency Medical Services
EMT	Emergency Medical Technician
FACE	Fatality Assessment and Control Evaluation
HSEES	Hazardous Substances Emergency Events Surveillance
IAFF	International Association of Fire Fighters
LEOKA	Law Enforcement Officers Killed and Assaulted
NaSH	National Surveillance System for Health-Care Workers
NCID	National Center for Infectious Diseases
NEISS	National Electronic Injury Surveillance System
NEMSMS	National EMS Memorial Service
NFIRS	National Fire Incident Reporting System
NFPA	National Fire Protection Association
NIOSH	National Institute for Occupational Safety and Health
NLEOMF	National Law Enforcement Officers Memorial Fund
NPPTL	National Personal Protective Technology Laboratory
NPSIB	National Public Safety Information Bureau
PASS	Personal Alert Safety System
R&D	Research and Development
SOC	Standard Occupation Classification
SOII	Survey of Occupational Injuries and Illnesses
USFA	United States Fire Administration

Executive Summary

The emergency response community represents a significant population of workers exposed to a particularly intense and variable hazard environment in the course of their work activities. This study focuses on firefighting, law enforcement, and emergency medical services personnel. In the United States, approximately 1,100,000 firefighters, 600,000 patrol and investigative law enforcement officers, and 500,000 emergency medical service responders answer calls for assistance and service that result in significant numbers of occupational injuries and fatalities.

In addition to the tragic events of September 11, in which over 400 emergency responders were killed, an average of 97 firefighters and 155 police officers died each year between 1990 and 2001, and an average of at least 11 nonfirefighter EMS personnel died in the line of duty each year between 1998 and 2001. The injury and fatality rates here and in the rest of this document do not include the events of September 11 because the magnitude of those tragic events obscures other trends in the data. The fatality rate for both police and career (paid) firefighters is approximately three times as great as the average for all occupations, placing them in the top fifteen occupations for the risk of fatal occupational injury; the fatality rate for emergency medical services responders is about two and one-half times the rate for all occupations. The rate of occupational injury and illness for employees of local fire and police agencies is similarly elevated. Approximately 88,000 firefighters are injured each year; about 2,000 of their injuries are potentially life-threatening. Approximately 100,000 police were injured in 2000.

This report is designed to collect and synthesize available data on casualties experienced by the emergency responder population for the purpose of estimating the frequency, causes, and characterization of those casualties.

The available data sources provide information about the occupational injuries and fatalities experienced by a significant portion of the emergency response community. Although there are some gaps in the data, many of these gaps are in the process of being addressed, and currently available data sources—in combination with community interviews and other sources of information—are adequate to provide an overview of emergency responder protection needs. In addition, extensive data are available to describe the injuries and fatalities suffered by firefighters. From these sources, counts and incidence rates are available for both fatalities and injuries, and both can be broken down by nature, cause, activity, and type of duty. The detailed National Fire Incident Reporting System (NFIRS) database, maintained by the U.S. Fire Administration, can be used to investigate specific questions about the risks faced by firefighters at fire scenes.

A lesser, but still useful, amount of information is available for police casualties. Significant data exist describing police fatalities, but less information is available on injuries. Detailed breakdowns of injuries from the Survey of Occupational Injuries and Illnesses (SOII), maintained by the Bureau of Labor Statistics, can be used to investigate specific questions about the risks faced by police officers. Information regarding officer activity at the time of injury is not available and represents the most significant gap in police data. Emergency medical services data sources are scarce, and few conclusions can be drawn from the existing data. However, some data are available describing fatalities, nature and body part of injury, and potential exposures to infectious diseases.

Improvements to the occupation coding used by the federal government that are currently underway will allow emergency medical responders to be broken out of government public health databases. In addition, the new categories for law enforcement responders will make understanding the hazards faced by officers involved in emergency response more straightforward. The SOII will become a particularly useful data source when these changes are implemented beginning in the 2003 data year.

The injuries most frequently experienced by firefighters are traumatic injuries, cuts and bruises, burns, asphyxiation and other respiratory injuries, and thermal stress. Physical stress and overexertion, falls, being struck by or making contact with objects, and exposure to fire products are the primary causes of injury at the fire scene. Physical stress, becoming lost or trapped in a fire situation, and vehicle accidents are the primary causes of death. Physical stress is responsible for nearly half of all on-duty deaths.

Approximately half of all firefighter injuries occur at the scene of fire emergencies, or "on the fireground." Firefighters experience a much higher risk of injury on the fireground than at other emergency incidents or during nonemergency duty. The injury incidence matrix shown in Figure S.1 shows graphically during which combinations of fireground activities and hazards firefighters are most often seriously injured, as well as the injuries that are most likely to result from each combination. Black cells correspond to combinations of

Cause of Injury

Firefighter Injuries	Fell, jumped	Caught, trapped	Struck by or contact with object	Exposure to fire products	Exposure to chemicals	Physical stress, over-exertion
Fire attack, search and rescue	Trauma Cuts/bruises	Burns Trauma	Cuts/bruises Trauma Burns	Burns Respiratory Heat stress	Respiratory	Trauma Heat stress Cardiac Respiratory
Ventilation and forcible entry	Trauma		Cuts/bruises Trauma	Respiratory Heat stress		Trauma Heat stress
Salvage and overhaul	Trauma		Cuts/bruises Trauma			Trauma Heat stress Cardiac
Incident scene support activities	Trauma Cuts/bruises		Cuts/bruises			Trauma Heat stress Cardiac
Riding on or driving apparatus	Trauma		Trauma Cuts/bruises Burns			Trauma

Fireground activity (vertical axis label)

■ Highest incidence ■ High incidence ■ Moderate incidence □ Low incidence

SOURCE: Based on data from the NFIRS 1998 Firefighter Casualty Module.

NOTES: Black cells indicate at least 150 reported injuries (10 percent of the total); dark-gray cells 36 to 66 injuries (2 to 4 percent); and light-gray cells 15 to 28 injuries (1 to 2 percent). Injuries with cause or activity unreported or reported as "other" are not included. Because of sample size, differences between some dark-gray and light-gray and some light-gray and white cells may not be statistically significant. Incident scene support activities include water supply operations and picking up and moving tools.

RAND *TR100-S.1*

Figure S.1—Injury Incidence Matrix for Moderate and Severe Firefighter Fireground Injuries by Cause and Activity

activities and hazards with the highest incidence of injuries, dark gray to high incidence, light gray to moderate incidence, and white to low incidence. Within each cell, the most common injuries are listed, with the most frequent injuries listed first.

The highest number of injuries from all causes occurs during fire attack and search and rescue. Fire attack is not only one of the most dangerous fireground activities but also one of the most common. In activities other than fire attack, firefighters are injured most frequently from falls during salvage and overhaul, incident scene support activities, or from apparatus; and from physical stress and overexertion or being struck by or making contact with an object during ventilation, forcible entry, salvage and overhaul, and incident scene support activities.

Cuts and bruises and traumatic injuries such as sprains, strains, and fractures are the most commonly encountered. Burns, respiratory trouble, and heat stress are also common injuries in "forward" activities such as fire attack and search and rescue.

Most injuries to police are traumatic injuries and cuts and bruises resulting from vehicle accidents, falls, assaults, or physical stress. Nine out of ten line-of-duty deaths are due to vehicle accidents or assaults. Figure S.2 compares the incidence of lost-time injuries to patrol and investigative officers from several types of hazards. As with the firefighter injury incidence matrix, black cells correspond to hazards resulting in the most injuries, dark gray to high incidence, light gray to moderate incidence, and white to low incidence.

Police are most often injured in falls, assaults, vehicle-related accidents, and through stress or overexertion. The most common injuries from all causes are traumatic injuries, such as sprains and strains, and cuts and bruises. Police are also at risk of burns and symptoms of illness as a result of exposure to fire and hazardous substances (in the figure, "illness" indicates injuries in which disease or illness symptoms are present but a definite diagnosis is lacking or is unclassifiable). These exposure-related injuries represent less than 1 percent of all law enforcement injuries.

Information about EMS injuries and hazards is scarce and far less definitive. EMS personnel are most at risk of sprains and strains, and back injuries represent a higher proportion of injuries for EMS personnel than they do for other

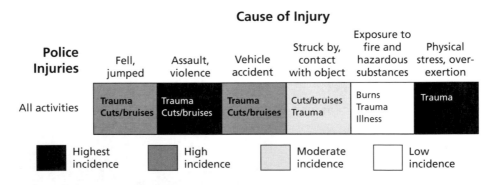

SOURCE: Based on data from the Survey of Occupational Injuries and Illnesses, Bureau of Labor Statistics (2003b).

NOTES: Data are for police and detectives, State of New York, at the local government level, for the years 1998–2000. Black cells represent at least 5,000 injuries; dark-gray cells at least 4,000 injuries; and the light-gray cell about 2,400 injuries. SOII estimates a total of 25,000 injuries for 1998–2000; the estimate in the figure is based on a smaller number of recorded cases.

RAND TR100-S.2

Figure S.2—Injury Incidence Matrix for Police Lost Work Time Injuries, by Cause

responders. EMS personnel also have a high risk of infectious disease exposure, mostly through percutaneous injuries such as needle sticks. Nearly all on-duty deaths for which data are available are due to aircraft and vehicle accidents.

The surveillance data clearly show that some hazards are common to all responders, including the risk of vehicle-related deaths, traumatic injuries such as sprains and strains, and cuts and bruises. The data also demonstrate the clear differences in hazard exposure and, consequently, the protection needs of segments of the emergency response community. The available data can provide a route for identifying those combinations of kinds and causes of injury, body parts involved, and types of responder activity where injury reduction efforts might be most effectively applied. Such detailed analyses are most accessible for firefighters because of the comparative richness of the available data sources.

However, injury counts alone are not sufficient to fully define the protection needs of emergency responders. By definition, they measure the negative consequences of exposure to particular risks over particular time periods. As a result, surveillance data give a preferential focus to routine activities because those tasks occupy the vast majority of responders' time. Therefore, the levels of injury should not be interpreted as direct measures of the level of risk faced by responders for *all* activities. Activities performed by responders for short periods of time, or events that occur infrequently, may involve a level of risk much higher than more common tasks. Natural disasters, major hazardous materials emergencies, structural collapse, civil disturbance, bomb disposal, hostage situations, and terrorism response all involve intense hazards not normally encountered in routine activities. The consequences of other potential hazards that have not yet been realized, such as large-scale terrorist attacks involving biological or chemical weapons, cannot be effectively captured. To fully assess responders' personal protection needs, all high-risk nonroutine activities must be considered separately from routine activities.

Similarly, while direct counts of injuries and the severity measures discussed in this report are excellent indicators of the scope of a health and safety problem, they cannot completely capture all the issues associated with the problem. For instance, although sprains and strains are the most common injuries experienced by responders in all three services, responders typically do not view these injuries as a primary concern. Thus, merely using injury frequencies when setting priorities for protective technology will not adequately address the concerns of the community. To address the limitations of a purely data-based approach, RAND has also gathered information directly from the emergency response community through an extensive structured-interview process. The results of that effort, included in a separate report (LaTourrette et al., 2003), are a critical complement to the surveillance data analyzed here.

Beyond simply demonstrating the utility of the currently available data and data sources, this analysis also suggests a range of potential future efforts that could contribute to a better understanding of this technology area. The diversity of data sources on emergency responders suggests that efforts to interconnect information from different databases could be valuable. An area of particular potential is fatality data—where the comparatively small number of cases and the availability of rich narrative information could enable many types of analysis. Such interconnection, combined with improved occupational coding efforts, would make it possible to ask detailed questions about protective technology design and performance in specific response situations.

1. Introduction

Every day in the United States, emergency responders answer calls for help and take on duties that place them in harm's way. Over two million paid and volunteer emergency responders play a critical role in protecting the American public and property from fire, natural disaster, medical emergency, and the actions of criminals and terrorists. As they fulfill their responsibilities, responders are exposed to significant risk of injury, illness, and death as part of their day-to-day jobs.

Responders accept that their job is hazardous—reflected in their principle of "risking a life to save a life"—but this acceptance does not diminish the importance of taking steps to protect them from the hazards inherent in their activities, including the development, deployment, and continued improvement of personal protective technology.

The National Institute for Occupational Safety and Health (NIOSH) National Personal Protective Technology Laboratory (NPPTL) asked the RAND Science and Technology Policy Institute to review available databases that provide disease, injury, and fatality data pertinent to emergency response functions and the role of personal protective technology. This report summarizes the results of an analysis of available surveillance data sources describing emergency responder injuries and fatalities. The analysis, along with the interests and concerns of the emergency responder community, is intended to support development of potential objectives and related research tasks directed at providing personal protective technologies to emergency responders.

Methodology

RAND obtained injury and fatality information from four responder community organizations and six federal agencies. This information included articles and other published reports, tabular data, sortable data sets, and complete sets of fatality data accompanied by narrative information. We identified data sources and cognizant organizations through recommendations from the emergency response community (including both emergency responders and research and support agencies),[1] recommendations from administrators of the data sources, federal government health and occupational health databases, and internet and literature searches. Pursuant to technical direction from NIOSH, we did not examine workers' compensation and insurance industry data sources.

For the analysis in this report, we used data from eight of these organizations, including all four of the responder community sources. This document does not distinguish occupational illness from occupational injury. This methodology parallels the approach taken in the injury epidemiology literature by analyzing injury and illness similarly; the primary difference between the two is the longer period of latency before the effects of an illness manifest themselves.[2] The fatalities resulting from the events of September 11 are not included because their inclusion would overwhelm other trends in the data.

Many of the data sources have restrictions that limit access to their most detailed data for privacy or other reasons. It is possible to get access to most of the restricted data with confidentiality agreements; these agreements typically require the administrating agency to review any documents produced that include the data. To avoid this problem, we chose to limit ourselves to publicly available information from restricted sources whenever such public information was adequate for our purposes. Because the analysis summarized in this report contributes to a larger effort sponsored by NPPTL that has resulted in several documents as well as informal communication of that information, we feel that our goal of providing timely and meaningful continuing contributions to NPPTL and to others in the emergency responder community is best served by eschewing confidential data wherever publicly available data are of comparable quality.

Any data access restrictions are discussed in the descriptions of individual data sources. Pursuing access to the confidential data could be an element of future analytical efforts in this area. Access to these data could provide a higher resolution understanding of injury incidence within some sectors of the responder population, particularly for law enforcement responders.

In order to have a single set of categories for nature, cause, activity, and type of duty, we did some reclassification, regrouping, and interpolation of data. Each

---

[1] The term *emergency response community* is used in this document to refer not only to emergency responders and their departments but also to technology providers and manufacturers, organizations, nongovernment research and data collection organizations, and other interested parties. The term *emergency responder population* is used to refer to the responders only. For this study, *emergency responders* are defined as members of the fire, law enforcement, and emergency medical services who respond to calls for service.

[2] See, for example, Haddon (1980).

data source has a distinct classification system for subcategorizing injuries and/or fatalities by nature, cause, and other factors. We made reasonable assumptions to translate these varied classification systems to a single system for all sources. Although this makes it possible to take advantage of a range of data sources on responder injuries and fatalities, the combined values do not linearly correspond to those reported in the individual data sources. Appendix A shows how the data sets were combined and explains where additional analysis was used to complete some categories. When multiple years or sets of data were collected within a single source, we combined the raw counts. For sources that reported only percentages, we estimated raw counts and combined the estimated counts. In the absence of clear reasons to select one data source over another, whenever two or more data sources used for analysis reported breakdowns by the same factor, we used the average of the sources. We weighted all sources equally.

The analysis in this document seeks to present the types of injuries and fatality experienced by emergency responders and the circumstances surrounding these casualties (cause of injury or death and type of activity). Where possible, we also did cross-analyses between nature and injury circumstance for firefighters and police. Our analysis of fatality data generally made use of complete or near-complete samples. Injury data were drawn primarily from surveys of either random or self-selected populations. As a result, uncertainty is inherent in the data, and small differences should not automatically be considered significant. All relative comparisons explicitly made in the text should be considered statistically significant. Statistical significance for such comparisons has been confirmed at a 95% confidence level or greater by a chi-square test (for sources providing exact counts in the surveillance sample), by a t test (for sources providing estimated counts or relative frequency but not exact counts for six or more independent sample years), by confidence interval bounds reported in the data source (for sources providing them), or by observation that the comparison would pass a chi-square test based on sample size and resolution (for all other sources).

About This Document

Section 2 describes the emergency responder population and characterizes the number and role of emergency responders in the United States. Section 3 describes the data sources that are available from responder community and government organizations, including the types of data contained in each source and how they can be used in analysis of responder injuries for personal protective technology program planning. Section 4 presents an analysis of the types of injuries experienced by emergency responders and the causes of injury and activities that put responders at risk. Section 5 presents our conclusions.

This report relates to Task B in the Interagency Project Description describing the work RAND is performing for NIOSH/NPPTL. Task B includes activities focused on helping NPPTL develop an agenda for its programs in personal protective technology research and development, partnership, service, and communication. This document serves as a deliverable relating to Task B1, "Analysis of Occupational Injury and Disease Data."

2. The Emergency Responder Population

Emergency responders are typically divided into three services: firefighters, police, and emergency medical services (EMS). We use this convention to define the emergency responder population. However, this division is neither complete nor comprehensive because many individual responders belong to more than one service and there is some variation in the duties of personnel within each service. For example, a firefighter may be cross-trained as an emergency medical technician and respond to medical calls, and a police officer may also serve as a volunteer firefighter. Furthermore, data sets (addressing both the responder population and injury incidence) do not have a uniform definition for who belongs to these services. Such definitional matters have an impact on how emergency responders are counted and how data about the risks they face are tallied and analyzed. An example of this can be seen with hazardous materials (hazmat) personnel: While the hazmat function is often provided by the fire service, in many places hazmat responders are either independent or part of the law enforcement group, and most of the responder community considers hazmat to be a separate function, similar to EMS: a function often (but frequently not) performed by the fire department but having distinct personnel and skills. However, the surveillance and population data sets we are aware of do not count hazmat personnel separately from their fire, police, or other affiliation.

Firefighters

The main division within the fire service is between career (paid) and volunteer firefighters and their respective fire departments. In general, most volunteer firefighters belong to smaller suburban and rural departments, whereas career firefighters belong to larger, urban departments. Because of the differences in type of jurisdiction, department size, and ability to provide specialized services, career firefighters experience a somewhat different range of hazards than volunteers do.[1]

---

[1] For example, the fraction of line-of-duty deaths that occur while responding to calls is much greater for volunteer firefighters because they typically respond to the scene or to the station in a personal vehicle and rural departments have geographically larger coverage zones, so more time is spent on the road. See NFPA (1995–2000a).

Each year, the National Fire Protection Association (NFPA) conducts a survey of municipal fire departments and estimates the number of firefighters. In 2000, 26,354 departments had a total complement of about 286,800 career firefighters and 777,350 active volunteer firefighters, for a total of about 1,054,000 firefighters. The career total constitutes all firefighters regardless of assignment, including some who are not directly involved in firefighting operations.

The 3,285 career or mostly career departments covered 62 percent of the country's population; 23,069 volunteer or mostly volunteer departments covered the remainder. The total number of municipal firefighters has remained nearly constant since 1985 at between 1.0 and 1.1 million, whereas the number of paid firefighters has been increasing steadily over the same period. State and federal governments (which employ many wildland firefighters) and private fire brigades are not included in this number. More than half of all departments provided some type of emergency medical service to the community.[2]

The National Public Safety Information Bureau (NPSIB) also publishes a yearly directory of fire and EMS departments. The 2002 directory lists 28,579 fire departments with about 1,446,000 total firefighting and EMS personnel, including 980,000 "firefighters" and 465,000 "emergency personnel." Some departments reported cross-trained firefighters and firefighting personnel who also responded to medical calls as "firefighters"; other departments reported them as "emergency personnel."[3] Both the NFPA and NPSIB numbers may overestimate the absolute number of firefighters, since career firefighters may volunteer in one or more departments, and volunteers can also belong to multiple departments.

Police/Law Enforcement

Of the three services, the total number of personnel in law enforcement is the easiest to count. However, the day-to-day roles of these personnel vary considerably. In addition to patrol officers, detectives, and others who are "on the street," sworn law enforcement personnel include bailiffs, correctional officers, and others who are unlikely to be on the front lines as emergency responders. Although police are actually a subset of all law enforcement officers, we use the terms interchangeably in this report.

---

[2] Karter (2001).

[3] NPSIB (2002a) and conversations with NPSIB staff.

The Bureau of Justice Statistics (BJS) periodically takes a census of law enforcement personnel at the state and local levels and surveys the number of personnel at the federal, state, and local levels. From these data, BJS calculates the number of personnel involved in patrol and investigation. Table 2.1 shows these data for 2000, the most recent year for which counts for both federal and state/local officers are available.

Table 2.1
Full-Time Law Enforcement Personnel, 2000

	Full-Time Sworn Personnel	Full-Time Nonsworn Personnel	Full-Time Sworn Personnel Who Respond to Calls for Service or Have Investigative Responsibility	
			Service	Investigative
Federal	88,496	72,000	17,000	36,000
State/local	708,022	311,474	424,000	106,000
Total	796,518	383,000	441,000	142,000

SOURCES: Reaves and Hart (2001), Reaves and Hickman (2002).

NOTE: Data on assignment are derived from percentages reported in the sources and are rounded to the nearest thousand.

In 2000, there were nearly 800,000 full-time sworn law enforcement officers, of whom about 441,000 regularly responded to calls for service and another 142,000 had primarily investigative responsibility. This number includes not only federal, state, city, and county governments but also special law enforcement departments, such as transit and campus police with (usually) firearm and arrest authority. Private-sector security professionals and employees of the military are not included. In addition, there were more than 380,000 full-time non-sworn or "civilian" employees. (The approximately 100,000 part-time personnel are not included in the table.)

Almost three-fourths of sworn personnel (the approximately 583,000 full-time officers with patrol or investigative responsibility) can be considered emergency responders, because their jobs require responding to incidents and dealing with a wide range of known and unknown hazards. The remaining full-time sworn personnel have some other primary responsibility, such as administrative, court, or correctional duties, and as a result face a more well-defined—but, in many cases, still significant—set of hazards.

The number of federal, state, and local officers, particularly those without emergency response duties, has been increasing steadily over the past ten years. The number of state and local full-time sworn officers increased 19 percent from 1990 to 2000, and the number of federal officers has increased 28 percent from 1993 to 2000.[4]

Emergency Medical Services

In a particular jurisdiction, emergency medical response may be the responsibility of a the local fire department, a separate "third service" public agency, a hospital or group of hospitals, a private company, or a combination of several of these organizations. In part because of the diversity among EMS organizations, no reliable counts of the number of EMS personnel exist. There are, however, several ways to estimate their number.

Members of the emergency response community have estimated their number from 100,000 to 1 million, with most estimates clustering around 500,000,[5] not including firefighters who respond regularly to both fire and medical emergencies.[6]

In addition, NPSIB data provide a range for the EMS population, and counts of paid EMS personnel and state-level EMS certifications are available. Taken together, these sources suggest that 500,000 is a reasonable estimate for the number of active EMS responders.

According to the 2002 NPSIB directory, about 212,000 emergency medical personnel belonged to EMS agencies (both public and private) and up to 465,000 belonged to fire departments (both career and volunteer), for a total range of 212,000 to 678,000 emergency medical responders.[7]

One statistic that is available is the number of EMS certifications. There were over 850,000 state-level EMS certifications in 2001 and possibly as many as

---

[4] Counts for 1990 and 1993 from Reaves (1992, 1994).

[5] Conversations with local and national firefighting and EMS organizations.

[6] In 2000, firefighters responded to more than 20 million calls, including about 1.7 million fire incidents and over 12 million emergency medical calls. See NFPA (2002).

[7] NPSIB (2002a).

1,000,000.[8] EMS certifications at the state level are required for practicing emergency medical responders. However, the number of EMS responders is much smaller, both because some individuals may be certified in multiple states and because the count of certified personnel includes firefighters and police, as well as people not affiliated with the emergency response community.

Like the fire service, EMS personnel are a combination of career and volunteer responders, as the affiliation information for National Registry Emergency Medical Technicians (EMTs) in Table 2.2 shows.[9] Paid emergency medical service personnel may belong to either public or private organizations. In 2001, the Bureau of Labor Statistics estimates that there were about 171,000 paid EMTs and paramedics.[10]

Responders with higher certifications, such as EMT-Paramedic, were more likely to belong to a paid public or private EMS service than were responders with only EMT-Intermediate or EMT-Basic certification. For all levels of certification,

Table 2.2
Affiliation of National Registry EMTs by Level of Certification, 1999 (%)

Level of Certification	Hospital–Based	Fire Department–Based	Municipal or County–Based	Private Ambulance Service	Volunteer Rescue Service
EMT Basic	15	24	14	14	33
EMT Intermediate	16	25	20	21	18
EMT Paramedic	18	31	17	28	5

SOURCE: National Registry of Emergency Medical Technicians (1999).
NOTE: Survey responses of other, unknown, or no response are omitted from the percentages reported in the table.

---

[8] *EMS Magazine* (2001) reports a total of about 877,000 certifications. However, about one-half of the states did not report the number of "first responder" certifications, and several states included dispatchers and emergency room doctors and nurses in the total. Excluding emergency room personnel and dispatchers, the total number of emergency responder certifications reported was about 860,000. This number includes about 140,000 paramedics, 575,000 basic and intermediate EMTs, and 145,000 first responders (for the states that reported first responder counts). If first responder certifications are roughly proportional to state population, an additional 140,000 emergency responder certifications were held in the states that did not report these counts.

[9] National Registry EMT certification is a nationwide certification that is recognized by many states through reciprocity agreements. The affiliation of National Registry EMTs may differ from the affiliation of state-certified EMTs.

[10] Bureau of Labor Statistics (2003a).

responders were distributed among hospital-based, fire department–based, municipal, and private organizations, with a significant number belonging to each type of organization.

3. Available Surveillance Data Sources to Define the Occupational Injury and Disease Characteristics of the Emergency Responder Workforce

Four main types of data sources provide information on the occupational hazards, injuries, and illnesses faced by emergency responders: responder-specific sources, incident-specific sources, general population occupational health and safety sources, and focused epidemiological studies.

- Responder-specific sources are generally collections of injury, fatality, and sometimes illness information for a single service. Because the format of the data can be tailored to focus specifically on the unique range of hazards faced by that service, the information can be very detailed.

- Incident-specific databases derive from reporting of specific types of incidents, in which responder injuries are only one part of the required reporting.

- General population data sets on work-related injuries, illnesses, and fatalities can be used to analyze emergency responder health and safety issues when the data sets contain occupation coding. Currently, such sources allow limited breakouts of data for police and firefighters, but usually not for EMS personnel.

- Focused studies, usually conducted by individual researchers or small groups, generally consider one or more safety and health problems. Such studies frequently use a small sample population, such as one state or a small number of departments, and generally address a specific type of occupational health hazard. Because non-acute occupational injuries and illnesses are not captured effectively in most data sets, researchers have conducted epidemiological studies to investigate these hazards. Firefighters are studied much more often than other emergency responders are. Focused studies have been done on such topics as the incidence and severity of hearing loss among Houston EMS workers[1] and the cancer incidence among firefighters in several Seattle-area fire departments.[2] Available studies suggest that there may be some elevated incidence of several types of cancer, hearing loss, respiratory problems, and other diseases among firefighters. The studies are frequently inconclusive, and indications of slightly increased risk are often present but not at statistically significant levels. One major complication in epidemiological studies is the "healthy worker effect." This manifests itself in two main ways. First, the population of emergency responders is healthier than the general population at the time of hiring because of the stringent fitness requirements for duty. Second, workers who become unfit after employment because of illness or exposure to occupational hazards may be removed from the workplace or reassigned to other duties and are often lost to follow-up analysis.[3]

RAND obtained data from four responder community organizations and six federal agencies (or obtained these reports online) and received a variety of data, including articles and other published reports, tabular data (frequently contained in published reports), sortable data sets, and narrative information. Available data on fatalities typically cover all fatalities, whereas data on injuries cover a subset of the total (either a random or self-selected sample).

This report uses data from eight of these organizations, including all of the community sources. Our review indicates that the various data sources have different inclusion criteria and different methods of classifying such information as cause and nature of injury. Even complete samples of the same nominal population are slightly different. The reasons for these differences include varying inclusion criteria—particularly those related to who is considered a responder and what constitutes an occupational fatality. For example, heart attacks occurring on duty are not considered occupationally related by several sources, whereas other sources include both on-duty heart attacks and those believed to be caused by an on-duty event. The following sections describe in detail the data sources we investigated, grouped by responder service.

---

[1] Pepe et al. (1985).

[2] Demers, Heyer, and Rosenstock (1992).

[3] Guidotti (1995).

Fire Service Sources

IAFF Death and Injury Survey

The International Association of Fire Fighters (IAFF)[4] *Death and Injury Survey* is an annual report based on a survey of a population-stratified random sample of career-only and career and/or volunteer fire departments. In a typical year, the sampled departments employ around 100,000 firefighters. Information collected includes line-of-duty deaths and injuries, incidence and type of infectious disease exposure, and occupational injury and illness retirements. Injuries are broken down by type of duty and nature of injury. IAFF provided RAND with this information for 1993–1998.

The *Death and Injury Survey* is the only firefighter data source that reports information regarding the incidence of infectious disease exposure and the causes of occupational injury and illness retirements. It has several limitations: First, it covers only career firefighters. Second, the injury breakdowns are given as a percentage of all injuries, not as raw or estimated counts. Thus it is somewhat difficult to make year-to-year comparisons, to compare the incidence of infectious disease exposure with other injuries and illnesses, and to do other analyses that requires data manipulation. It is IAFF policy, however, not to provide raw counts.

NFPA Firefighter Injury Reports

The National Fire Protection Association[5] produces an annual report of firefighter injuries based on a survey of a population-stratified random sample of municipal (city and county) fire departments. In 2000, nearly 3,000 fire departments, protecting 37 percent of the U.S. population, responded to the survey. The report is published each year in the *NFPA Journal*.[6] NFPA estimates the total number of firefighter line-of-duty injuries in the nation, broken down by type of duty and nature of injury for all injuries (including a crosswalk of both variables), as well as by cause of injury for fireground injuries. NFPA provided RAND with this information for 1995–2000.

---

[4] International Association of Fire Fighters, 1750 New York Ave, NW, Washington, DC 20006 (http://www.iaff.org/).

[5] National Fire Protection Association, 1 Batterymarch Park, Quincy, MA 02269 (http://www.nfpa.org/Home/index.asp).

[6] Sample reference: Michael J. Karter and Paul LeBlanc, "U.S. Firefighter Injuries— – 1996," *NFPA Journal*, Vol. 91, No. 6, November/December 1997, pp. 67–77.

The NFPA firefighter injury reports cover both career and volunteer firefighters, effectively complementing the IAFF *Death and Injury Survey* by providing much of the same information but for the total firefighter population instead of career firefighters only. Together, the two sources permit a qualitative comparison of career and volunteer firefighter injuries.

NFPA Firefighter Fatality Reports

NFPA also produces an annual report on firefighter fatalities in the *NFPA Journal*.[7] The NFPA firefighter fatality reports break down the complete set of on-duty deaths by nature of injury, cause of injury, type of duty, and other factors, such as demographics and type of property for fireground deaths, as well as the relationship between these factors. NFPA provided RAND with this information for 1995–2000.

Also valuable are analyses of special topics in each annual report. These more detailed studies include deaths associated with incendiary and suspicious fires (1995), analysis of deaths while responding to or returning from alarms (1996), and fatalities among firefighters wearing Personal Alert Safety System (PASS) devices (1997).

USFA Firefighter Fatality Reports

The United States Fire Administration (USFA) also produces an annual report based on the complete set of firefighter on-duty deaths. Fatalities are broken down by nature of injury and cause of injury; and type of duty, fireground activity, and other factors such as demographics and type of property for fireground deaths. In addition, the report contains narrative information describing the circumstances of every fatality. Special topics, such as homicides and violence in the workplace, firefighter health and wellness, and vehicle accidents (1996 report) are also covered. For the analysis in this document, we used reports for 1995–2000.[8]

This data source has significant overlap with the NFPA firefighter fatality reports. One advantage of the USFA database is that it includes narrative reports for all fatalities and a breakdown by activity for fireground injuries.

---

[7] Sample reference: Arthur E. Washburn, Paul R. LeBlanc, and Rita F. Fahy, "1996 Firefighter Fatalities," *NFPA Journal*, Vol. 91, No. 4, July/August 1997, pp. 46–60.

[8] Reports are available dating back to 1986 at http://www.usfa.fema.gov/dhtml/inside-usfa/ff_fat.cfm (accessed 10/31/02).

National Fire Incident Reporting System

The National Fire Incident Reporting System (NFIRS) is an incident-based database maintained by USFA that contains information on fire incidents reported by fire departments in 44 states. About one-third to one-half of all U.S. fire departments participate. The database contains information about the type of incident, amount of loss, and civilian and firefighter casualties. Extremely detailed information about firefighter injuries is available in the firefighter casualty module, including the nature, severity, and cause of injury; body part involved; activity at the time of injury; and type of personal protective equipment worn and whether it performed adequately. USFA provided RAND with the firefighter casualty module for 1998. The 1998 firefighter casualty module contains about 7,000 records, or about 8 percent of all firefighter injuries.[9] For 1998, the NFIRS database covered only fire incidents, but the NFIRS reporting system is being updated to include all emergency incidents to which fire departments respond, not only fire incidents. The database includes primarily fireground injuries, with few reported injuries for other types of duty; in 1998, about 95 percent of injuries in the casualty module occurred on the fireground.

NFPA has published a report, *Patterns of Firefighter Fireground Injuries*, which is an analysis of NFIRS data for 1993–1997 corresponding to fireground injuries only. The data are weighted by year based on information in NFPA's annual survey of fire departments, and unknown data were estimated based on the same proportional distribution as known data.[10] This process produces national estimates of the number and types of injuries and improves data quality by correcting for missing data, but the resulting data set is less flexible than the raw NFIRS data.

The NFIRS database is an extremely useful data source. The firefighter casualty module is a sortable database, so the records can be sampled to explore specific combinations and relationships between the nature and circumstance of injuries. Because the data are voluntarily reported, it is not known whether the reporting departments are representative of the fire service as a whole.[11]

---

[9] Total number of injuries from NFPA firefighter injury report (1998).

[10] Karter (2000).

[11] Hall and Harwood (1985).

Firefighter Fatality Investigation Reports

NIOSH's firefighter fatality investigation reports, part of the Fatality Assessment and Control Evaluation (FACE) Program, are detailed investigations into the causes and circumstances of a subset of firefighter fatality incidents. The reports also offer recommendations on preparedness, management, training, and other factors that might have prevented the casualties.[12]

Although these reports investigate only a subset of fatalities, the depth of the investigations makes them very useful as a connection between protective technology opportunities and the overall surveillance data analysis. The reports can be used to identify personal protective technology solutions that could reduce the number of injuries and fatalities from particular causes.

Law Enforcement Sources

National Law Enforcement Officers Memorial Fund Database

The National Law Enforcement Officers Memorial Fund (NLEOMF)[13] keeps a database of all line-of-duty deaths, broken down by "primary reason" (similar to cause of injury), whether the fatality was accidental or felonious, and other factors, mostly demographic. Short narratives contained in the database allow hand-coding of small samples.

This source is particularly useful because it is the only source that reports line-of-duty illness fatalities for law enforcement personnel. NLEOMF provided RAND with all records for 1992–2001.

Law Enforcement Officers Killed and Assaulted

Law Enforcement Officers Killed and Assaulted (LEOKA) is an annual statistical compilation concerning law enforcement officers who were feloniously or accidentally killed or assaulted in the line of duty, prepared by the FBI Uniform Crime Reporting System's Law Enforcement Officers Killed and Assaulted Program. It includes counts of all fatalities reported by law enforcement agencies contributing to the FBI Uniform Crime Reporting System—a somewhat smaller sample than the number reported by NLEOMF and the Census of Fatal

---

[12] The investigation reports may be found at http://www.cdc.gov/niosh/face/firerpts.html (accessed 10/30/02).

[13] National Law Enforcement Officers Memorial Fund, 400 7th Street, NW, Suite 300, Washington, DC 20004 (http://nleomf.org/index1.html).

Occupational Injuries (CFOI) (see below). LEOKA reports are available online from 1996 to 2000, although the database goes back further.[14]

LEOKA reports provide significant information concerning all aspects of felonious deaths, including narrative information, type of weapon, type of assignment, and distance between the officer and the offender. Comparatively little information is available for accidental deaths. Nonfatal assaults are broken down by type of weapon and extent of injury.

Emergency Medical Services Sources

National EMS Memorial Service Database

The National EMS Memorial Service (NEMSMS)[15] keeps a database of line-of-duty deaths, broken down by cause of death and containing some narrative information about the circumstances surrounding the death. Unlike the NFPA, USFA, and NLEOMF databases, NEMSMS depends entirely on nominations from the responder community to identify fatalities and compile this information. It is not known whether the fatality reports are a complete sample or are representative of the EMS population. RAND used data for 1998–2001 obtained from the NEMSMS website.

National Surveillance System for Health Care Workers

The National Surveillance System for Health Care Workers (NaSH), maintained by the National Center for Infectious Diseases, collects information on occupational exposures and infections among health-care workers, including hospital-based EMTs, in a small sample of hospitals (in 1999, there were 23 participating hospitals). For infectious disease exposures, the data include information about the mechanism of exposure. The Centers for Disease Control and Prevention (CDC) provided RAND with data from the program's inception in June 1995 through February 2002.

General Population or Multi-Service Sources

A particular strength of general population sources is that responders can be compared between services and to the general population using the same

---

[14] Reports may be found at http://www.fbi.gov/ucr/ucr.htm dating back to 1996 (accessed 10/31/02).

[15] National EMS Memorial Service, P.O. Box 279, Oilville, VA 23129 (ht tp://nemsms.org/).

reporting criteria. However, multiple-service sources also tend not to be as detailed as the responder-specific data sets because they are unable to focus on the specific range of hazards faced by emergency responders.

Census of Fatal Occupational Injuries

The Census of Fatal Occupational Injuries, maintained by the Bureau of Labor Statistics (BLS), provides counts of law enforcement and career firefighter work-related injury fatalities. Heart attacks and other non-traumatic on-duty injuries are not considered work-related. The fatalities are broken down by several factors. RAND has obtained these data for 1992–2000,[16] as well as a report summarizing the data for 1992–1997.[17] Another general population data source, the National Traumatic Occupational Fatalities Surveillance System, maintained by NIOSH, provides similar information.

In our analysis, CFOI was used only to compare the fatality rate of firefighters and police to the general population using a common set of selection criteria. Because of stringent confidentiality requirements, many of the cell counts that would be part of detailed breakdowns by variables of interest such as event/exposure and activity are not publicly available. Because of this, coupled with the fact that the NFPA, USFA, and NLEOMF databases include much more descriptive information, we did not pursue CFOI for detailed breakdowns of the nature and circumstance of line-of-duty fatalities.

Survey of Occupational Injuries and Illnesses

The Survey of Occupational Injuries and Illnesses (SOII), maintained by the Bureau of Labor Statistics, reports counts and incidence rates for occupational injuries, broken down by occupation. Occupation categories include firefighters (code 417), and police and detectives (code 418). Recordable injuries and illnesses are defined as occupational deaths, regardless of the time between injury and death or the length of the illness; nonfatal occupational illnesses; and nonfatal occupational injuries that involve one or more of the following: loss of consciousness, restriction of work or motion, transfer to another job, or medical treatment (other than first aid).

---

[16] Data received from BLS staff. Some data can also be obtained online at http://www.bls.gov/iif/oshcfoi1.htm (accessed 10/31/02).

[17] Clarke and Zak (1999).

Detailed breakdowns of the data are available from the Case and Demographic staff for injuries involving lost workdays. These data can be broken down by nature of injury, event/exposure (cause), part of body, and other factors. The records contain days away from work for each injury. In addition, the median days away from work can be reported for each injury category, providing a rough measure of relative severity.

Some SOII data on emergency responder injuries can be obtained online, broken down by industry.[18] Some states report the incidence counts and rates for local-government public administration: police protection (industry code 9221) and fire protection (code 9224). Civilian employees of public safety agencies are included in these counts. In 2000, these data were available for California, Maine, New Jersey, New York, and North Carolina.

A major limitation of this source for police and firefighter injuries (EMS personnel cannot be broken out) is that public-sector injury data are not aggregated above the state level. Information on injuries to public sector employees is reported by only some states,[19] and state and local governments are separated. Because of strict confidentiality requirements that prevent the publication of small cell counts, having a number of small data sets instead of one or two larger sets means that a significant portion of the data is not publicly available, and only California and New York local governments have enough case counts for reportable information to be available for any but the most simple breakdowns. Access to these data could presumably be obtained via agreement with the BLS or through the Bureau's standard process for obtaining researcher access to confidential data, although BLS confidentiality requirements may prevent the publication or dissemination of this information. BLS considers applications for this access three times a year.[20]

For the purpose of reviewing the SOII database, BLS provided RAND with complete breakdowns by nature, event/exposure, event/exposure and nature, and event/exposure and part of body (with mean days away from work for all breakdowns) for police and detectives at the local government level in New York state (the state reporting the most police injuries), for the years 1998–2000.

EMS workers are not broken out of SOII and most other general population databases because occupation and industry codes currently in use do not allow

---

[18] http://www.bls.gov/iif/oshstate.htm (accessed 10/31/02).

[19] Data for public-sector employees are available only for those states that have OSHA-approved safety programs; in 2000, there were 25 such states. Data from "non-OSHA" states are not available.

[20] John W. Ruser, Bureau of Labor Statistics, personal communication, 3/18/02.

them to be identified. However, revisions to the Standard Occupation Classification (SOC) System in 1998 created a category for emergency medical technicians and paramedics, and grouped law enforcement personnel into more-useful categories, including separating police and sheriff's patrol officers from officers who are likely not emergency responders.

NIOSH, BLS, and other government data sources with occupational coding are switching from Census 1980 codes based on the old SOC system to Census 2000 codes based on the 1998 SOC revision. Some sources have already transitioned, while others will do so over the new few years. As of October 15, 2002, no occupational injury data sources had made the transition. The BLS is expected to adopt the new occupation coding for year 2003 SOII data, which will be available in 2005. Table 3.1 shows the 1980–1990 occupation codes currently in use and the new 2000 codes.

National Electronic Injury Surveillance System

The most significant EMS injury data source that RAND was able to obtain was from the National Electronic Injury Surveillance System (NEISS) maintained by NIOSH, which utilizes data reported by a sample of hospital emergency departments. A NIOSH analysis done with 1996–1998 data investigated injuries to responders in all three emergency services, coding occupation from narrative information.[21] The analysis broke injuries down by nature of injury and part of body for all three services. These data are preliminary—the limited occupation information reported by NEISS does not allow accurate distinction between fire department employees injured while serving in a fire control capacity versus serving primarily as an EMT. Additionally, firearms-related injuries were are not included in the data set. Although the reported injury incidence rates and injury estimates may have some error as a result of occupation definition issues, the general proportions of injuries by nature and body part are not expected to change significantly. However, these preliminary data should be viewed judiciously because they may change with further analyses or injured-worker follow-back studies on workers' activity and occupation at the time of injury .[22]

National Occupational Mortality Surveillance System

The National Occupational Mortality Surveillance System, maintained by NIOSH, contains information on the cause of death and normal occupation

---

[21] NIOSH, L. L. Jackson, unpublished data.

[22] Larry Jackson, NIOSH, personal communication, 8/1/02.

Table 3.1—Occupation Codes Used in Federal Government Data Sources

Service	Census 1980 Codes	Census 2000 Codes
	Occupation Codes	
Police and other law enforcement	414 Supervisors, Police and Detectives[a]	370 First-Line Supervisors/ Managers of Correctional Officers
	415 Supervisors, Guards	371 First-Line Supervisors/ Managers of Police and Detectives[a]
	418 Police and Detectives, Public Service[a]	
	423 Sheriffs, Bailiffs, and Other Law Enforcement Officers	380 Bailiffs, Correctional Officers, and Jailers
	424 Correctional Institution Officers	382 Detectives and Criminal Investigators[a]
		383 Fish and Game Wardens
		384 Parking Enforcement Workers
		385 Police and Sheriff's Patrol Officers[a]
		386 Transit and Railroad Police[a]
Firefighters and other fire service	413 Supervisors, Firefighting and Fire Prevention Occupations[a]	372 First-Line Supervisors/ Managers of Fire Fighting and Prevention Workers[a]
	416 Fire Inspection and Fire Prevention Occupations	374 Fire Fighters[a]
	417 Firefighting Occupations[a]	375 Fire Inspectors
EMS	106 Physician's Assistants	340 Emergency Medical Technicians and Paramedics[a]
	207 Licensed Practical Nurses	
	208 Health Technologists and Technicians, not elsewhere classified	
	446 Health Aides, except Nursing	
	447 Nursing Aides, Orderlies, and Attendants	

SOURCE: Census 1980 occupation codes for EMS personnel from Maguire, et al. (2002)..

NOTES: The categories in the table are those in which emergency responders may be placed, or in which nonresponder fire department and police personnel are likely to be placed.

[a]Persons with this occupation code are likely to be emergency responders.

and industry of the deceased for a significant fraction of *all* deaths, not just those that are work-related. Frequencies and proportional mortality ratios for specific occupations can be computed. However, the data do not include genetic and behavioral risk factors such as smoking, many of which are likely more significant than occupational risk factors. As such, extensive modeling and analysis of responder and control populations would be required to use these data. We therefore did not pursue this data source for this analysis.

Hazardous Substances Emergency Events Surveillance

The Hazardous Substances Emergency Events Surveillance (HSEES), maintained by the Agency for Toxic Substances and Disease Registry, captures information about any incident involving the release or threatened release of at least one hazardous substance, where *hazardous* is defined as "might reasonably be expected to cause adverse human health effects." Releases of only petroleum products are excluded, and data are collected from participating states. Figure 3.1 shows the states reporting for 1998.

Information is included in the database on all injuries occurring at these events, including injuries to emergency responders. Responder injuries are broken down by type of responder, nature and severity of injury, and type of protective equipment worn. Counts of responder injuries and their nature and severity can

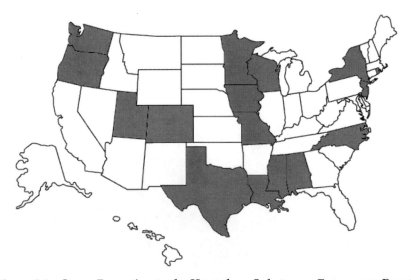

Figure 3.1—States Reporting to the Hazardous Substances Emergency Events Surveillance, 1998

be obtained from published Annual Reports, available online for 1995–1998.[23] More-detailed information can be requested directly from the Agency for Toxic Substances and Disease Registry.

Table 3.2 shows the data sources we obtained that contain information regarding the injuries, illnesses, and fatalities experienced by emergency responders. Although we did not use data from all of the cited sources in the overview of responder injuries and fatalities in the following section, all sources are included here as potential contributors to subsequent analyses.

Findings

Extensive data are available for firefighters. By combining sources, counts and incidence rates are available for both fatalities and injuries, and both can be broken down by nature, cause, activity and type of duty. For police, the data are less extensive, but still adequate to characterize the risks encountered by responders. Information on responder activity at the time of injury is not available and represents the largest gap in police data. For emergency medical responders, analogous data sources do not yet exist, but some information on fatalities, injuries, and infectious disease exposure is available. Improvements to occupation coding in federal government databases are currently underway which will provide new sources of information on EMS injuries.

Although there are some gaps in the data, currently available data sources are adequate to provide an overview of emergency responder protection needs. Table 3.3 summarizes the information currently available from all data sources to describe the injuries, illnesses, and fatalities experienced by emergency responders.

Information is also scarce for non–acute onset and chronic health effects. This problem is not unique to emergency responders. Because conditions with long latency periods and unclear connections to occupational activities are much more

---

[23] http://www.atsdr.cdc.gov/HS/HSEES/ (accessed 10/31/02).

Table 3.2
Major Data Sources Describing Emergency Responder Injuries and Fatalities

Data Source Name and Supporting Organization	Type and Services	Data Format	Years Used by RAND	Online Access?
Death and Injury Survey (IAFF)	Responder-specific (fire)	Tabular	1993–1998	No
Firefighter Fatality Reports (NFPA)	Responder-specific (fire)	Complete set tabular	1995–2001	No
Firefighter Injury Reports (NFPA)	Responder-specific (fire)	Tabular	1995–2000	No
Firefighter Fatality Reports (USFA)	Responder-specific (fire)	Complete set narrative, tabular	1995–2000	Yes
National Fire Incident Reporting System (USFA)	Incident-specific (fire)	Sortable	1998	No
Firefighter Fatality Investigation Reports (NIOSH)	Responder-specific (fire)	Narrative	—	Yes
National Law Enforcement Officers Memorial Fund	Responder-specific (police)	Complete set narrative, sortable	1992–2001	No
Law Enforcement Officers Killed and Assaulted (FBI)	Responder-specific (police)	Complete set tabular	—	Yes
National EMS Memorial Service	Responder-specific (EMS)	Narrative	1998–2001	Yes
National Surveillance System for Health Care Workers (NCID)	Responder-specific (EMS)	Tabular	1995–2002	No
Census of Fatal Occupational Injuries (BLS)	General population (fire, police)	Sortable by BLS staff	1992–1997	Yes
Survey of Occupational Injuries and Illnesses (BLS)	General population (fire, police)	Sortable by BLS staff	1998–2000	Yes
National Electronic Injury Surveillance System (NIOSH)	General population (all)	Tabular	1996–1998	No
National Occupational Mortality Surveillance (NIOSH)	General population (fire, police)	Tabular	—	No
Hazardous Substances Emergency Events Surveillance (ATSDR)	Incident-specific (all)	Tabular	—	Yes

Table 3.3
Coverage of the Data Describing Risks Faced by Emergency Responders

	Firefighters	Police	EMS
Fatal Injuries and Illnesses			
Counts or incidence rates	Yes	Yes	—
Nature and part of body	Yes	Narrative only	Narrative only
Cause or event/exposure	Yes	Yes	Yes
Type of duty and activity	Yes	Narrative only	Narrative only
Illness included?	Yes	Yes	Yes
Nonfatal Injuries and Illnesses			
Counts or incidence rates	Yes	Only lost time injuries for certain states	—
Severity	Yes	Yes	—
Nature and part of body	Yes	Yes	Yes
Cause or event/exposure	Yes	Yes	—
Type of duty and activity	Yes	—	—
Other Health and Safety Data			
Injury/illness retirements	Yes	—	—
Infectious disease exposure	Yes	—	Yes
Hazmat incidents	Yes	Yes	Yes

difficult to detect than acute injuries, they may be universally underreported. The extent of underreporting, however, is not known.[24] Although focused epidemiological studies provide one source for this information, the long-term health consequences of emergency response still represent an important gap in our understanding.

Firefighters

For firefighters, the available data sources are extensive. These sources provide information on the incidence rate and total number of on-duty injuries and fatalities; the relative prevalence and severity of injuries broken down by nature of injury, cause of injury, and the type of incident and type of activity at the time of injury; and narrative information for the complete set of firefighter fatalities. In addition, the firefighter injury and fatality data can be easily extrapolated to the entire firefighter population (this is less true for disease and non-acute injuries).

Table 3.4 shows this applicability of each part of the firefighter data to the entire population. This table is a not a commentary on the accuracy or reliability of any

---

[24] Murphy et al. (1996).

Table 3.4
Applicability of Casualty Data to Firefighter Population

Type of Data	Applicability	Comments
Fatal injury	Excellent	Multiple sources offering data with high or very high applicability (NFPA, USFA, IAFF)
Fatal illness	Excellent	Multiple sources offering data with high or very high applicability (NFPA, USFA, IAFF)
Nonfatal injury	Excellent	Multiple sources offering data with high or very high applicability (NFPA, IAFF, NFIRS)
Nonfatal illness	Low	Underreported in all sources;, cannot make any meaningful or significant conclusions
Injury/illness retirements	Excellent	Only for career firefighters; data from IAFF
Infectious disease exposure	Medium	Underreported in NFIRS; IAFF data include only career firefighters; does not have a standard definition of "exposure"
Hazmat incidents	High	HSEES provides data for participating states

particular data source—not all data sources are designed or intended to reflect the entire firefighter population.[25]

NFPA firefighter injury reports and the *Death and Injury Survey* both provide breakdowns of all on-duty injuries by nature and type of duty. In addition, the NFPA injury reports and NFIRS data provide breakdowns by the nature, cause, and firefighter activity for fireground injuries. The *Death and Injury Survey* also allows comparison between injuries and infectious disease exposures and documents the causes of occupational injury and illness retirements. The NFPA and USFA firefighter fatality reports provide information on the complete set of line-of-duty fatalities. These can be further supplemented with specific investigative results, such as those reported by the NIOSH Fire Fighter Fatality Investigation and Prevention Program.

The NFPA sources, the IAFF *Death and Injury Survey*, and USFA firefighter fatality reports are all useful for defining a framework to investigate the natures, causes, and types of activities most responsible for injuries and fatalities. For

---

[25] For example, the IAFF *Death and Injury Survey* looks only at casualties suffered by career firefighters, who constitute the IAFF membership. These data are somewhat less applicable to the entire (career and volunteer) population than are the NFPA firefighter injury reports, which include both types.

more-detailed analysis, the NFIRS database is extremely useful. The firefighter casualty module is a sortable database, so the records can be sampled to explore specific relationships between the nature and circumstance of injuries and to address other detailed questions about the hazards faced by firefighters.

Police/Law Enforcement

Although databases tracking the activities and injuries of law enforcement responders are less developed than those focusing on tracking crime and criminals, a significant amount of data is available describing police injuries and fatalities. A variety of sources provide narrative information for the complete set of line-of-duty fatalities. The National Law Enforcement Officers Memorial Fund database is particularly useful because it includes line-of-duty fatalities resulting from illnesses as well as traumatic events, and all data are publicly releasable. The FBI report, Law Enforcement Officers Killed and Assaulted, does not capture as many fatalities but does provide some information on nonfatal assaults, which result in a significant portion of job-related injuries.

Several data sources provide information on the nature and cause of nonfatal injuries. Of these sources, the most detailed data come from the BLS Survey of Occupational Injuries and Illnesses. However, because of confidentiality requirements and the fact that data for public-sector employees are not aggregated above the state level, fewer data are publicly available that describe nonfatal injuries to police officers than are available for workers in private industry (data for the latter are aggregated nationally). In the context of future analysis of responder injuries, researchers may be able either to fulfill the requirements needed to obtain access to the confidential records or to obtain already-analyzed data via an agreement with BLS. The SOII data are sortable by BLS staff, and can be used to address some detailed questions about the type and frequency of police injuries. Overall, the applicability of police data to the total responder population is high, as shown in Table 3.5. The largest hole in this regard is the nonfatal-injury data.

Aggregated injury and illness data for the reporting states would significantly upgrade the ability to compare injuries within and across all three services and the general population. Unlike firefighter data sources, no data source provides

Table 3.5
Applicability of Casualty Data to Law Enforcement Population

Type of Data	Applicability	Comments
Fatal injury	Excellent	Multiple sources offering data with high or very high applicability (NLEOMF, FBI)
Fatal illness	High	NLEOMF data include illness as well
Nonfatal injury	Medium	BLS data publicly available on a state-by-state basis only; only very large states have enough reported injuries to be useful for analysis
Hazmat incidents	High	HSEES provides data for participating states

information on officer activity at the time of injury. The ability to match injuries to responder activity would be greatly enhanced if worker activity was recorded and tabulated for BLS injury data using a scale similar to the one for fatality data in CFOI.

Emergency Medical Services

Data on EMS responders are scarce. Some narrative information is available to describe EMS line-of-duty fatalities, and the NaSH database and IAFF *Death and Injury Survey* describe the mechanism and type of disease for infectious disease exposures. Available data are difficult to extrapolate to the entire population, as indicated in Table 3.6. This difficultly is compounded by the fragmented nature of the EMS sector.

General-population sources contain information on police and firefighters, but EMS personnel are not typically broken out. However, an analysis of NEISS data made available to RAND by NIOSH researchers breaks injuries down by nature of injury and part of body involved for all three emergency response services, and allows the injuries to be compared across services.[26] This study, which is not publicly releasable, is the only source of information on EMS nonfatal injuries,

---

[26] L. L. Jackson, NIOSH, unpublished data.

Table 3.6
Applicability of Casualty Data to EMS Responder Population

Type of Data	Applicability	Comments
Fatal injury	Medium	NEMSMS data do not constitute a complete set; fewer data on reported fatalities than other services
Fatal illness	Medium	NEMSMS data do not constitute a complete set; fewer data on reported fatalities than other services
Nonfatal injury	Medium	NEISS data applicable at only the highest level no detailed information yet available (BLS data available beginning 2005)
Hazmat incidents	High	HSEES provides data for participating states

other than infectious disease exposures, we found. As a result, only very basic generalizations about EMS injuries can be made. However, changes in occupation coding for federal government data sources currently being implemented will enable researchers to break out injuries to emergency medical technicians and paramedics from SOII and other databases, increasing the amount of available EMS injury data. It is likely that once these changes are implemented, the quality and quantity of EMS injury data will be similar to those of law enforcement data.

4. Observations from the Data Regarding Risks Faced by Emergency Responders

Because of the high level of risk associated with their mission and responsibilities, emergency responders are subject to a significant number of occupational injuries, illnesses, and fatalities. In addition to the tragic events of September 11, in which over 400 responders lost their lives, an average of 97 firefighters and 155 police officers were killed in the line of duty each year from 1990 to 2001 (see Figure 4.1). The firefighter deaths include those that occur when firefighters are performing EMS duties, and an average of at least 11 additional non-firefighter emergency medical responders died in the line of duty each year between 1998 and 2001.[1] Excluding those associated with September 11, responder fatalities have decreased substantially from the level in the early 1980s, when over 300 responders died each year.

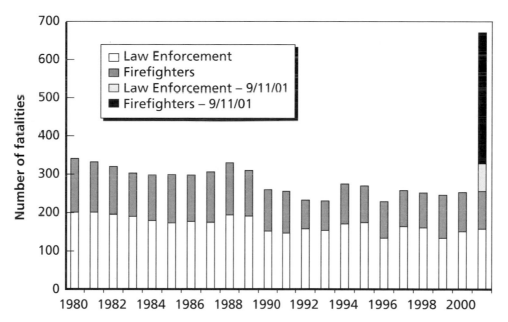

SOURCE: U.S. Fire Administration (2002), National Law Enforcement Officers Memorial Fund (2002b).

RAND TR100-4.1

Figure 4.1—Firefighter and Law Enforcement Fatalities, 1980–2001

---

[1] National EMS Memorial Service (2002).

However, no significant long-term improvement has occurred since 1990. (The deaths associated with September 11 are not treated in the discussion in this section because their inclusion would overwhelm other trends in the data.)

The fatality rate for both police[2] and career firefighters[3] is approximately three times as great as the average for all occupations and places them in the top fifteen occupations for the risk of fatal occupational injury.[4] The rate of occupational injury and illness for employees of local fire and police agencies is similarly elevated. For all but one of the states for which SOII injury data for 2000 are available online, both local police and fire department employees had injury rates higher than the average for all industries. In the most extreme case, the rate for fire department employees was more than seven times the state average for all workers and the rate for police department employees was nearly four times the state average (Table 4.1).

Table 4.1
Incidence Rates of Nonfatal Injuries and Illnesses per 100 Full-Time Emergency Responders for Five States, 2000

State	All Industries	Fire Protection	Relative Risk	Police Protection	Relative Risk
California	6.5	16.7	2.6	20.0	3.1
Maine	8.7	11.8	1.4	7.1	0.8
New Jersey	5.5	18.8	3.4	15.8	2.9
New York	4.7	34.8	7.4	18.2	3.9
North Carolina	5.3	NA	NA	9.4	1.8

SOURCE: Bureau of Labor Statistics (2002).

NOTES: Data are for police protection (industry code 9221) and fire protection employees (code 9224) at the local government level. The incidence rate represents the number of injuries and illnesses per 100 full-time workers. To adjust for occupations with a nonstandard amount of hours (such as firefighters), the incidence rate is calculated by multiplying the number of injuries and illnesses times the total hours worked by all employees during the calendar year and dividing that product by 200,000 (the base for 100 full-time equivalent workers working 40 hours per week, 50 weeks per year). Relative risk is defined as (injury and illness rate for given occupation)/ (injury and illness rate for all industries).

[2] The occupational fatality data presented in this section cover all law enforcement personnel, including those who are not emergency responders. The occupational injury data presented in this section cover only local government police and detectives (BLS data) or all law enforcement personnel (NEISS data).

[3] Firefighter injury and illness data presented in this section apply to all firefighters (both career and volunteer) unless explicitly indicated in the text as including only career firefighters. Injury and fatality rate data include only career firefighters because of the difficulty of determining hours worked for volunteers.

[4] The fatality rate per 100,000 workers in 1992–1997 was 16.5 for firefighters and 14.2 for police and detectives compared with a value of 5.0 for all occupations. See Clarke and Zak (1999).

Between 1995 and 2000, the U.S. firefighter population of more than one million (both career and volunteer) averaged 88,000 work-related injuries each year.[5] A similar number of injuries occurred for police: Extrapolating from the data in Table 4.1, in 2000 there were approximately 100,000 injuries and illnesses in the United States in a population of nearly 600,000 full time patrol and investigative officers.[6, 7]

EMS injury and fatality rate data are difficult to find. An investigation of National NEMSMS fatality data and the CFOI estimates the occupational fatality rate of EMS responders to be about 2.5 times the rate for all workers.[8] No information is available on the incidence rate of EMS injuries.

Within this discussion, we performed some reclassification, regrouping, and interpolation to produce a single set of categories for nature and cause of injury, responder activity, and type of duty. Each data source has a distinct classification system for subcategorizing injuries and/or fatalities by nature, cause, and other factors. We used reasonable assumptions to translate these various classification systems to a single system for all sources. Although a single system makes it possible to take advantage of a range of data sources on responder injuries and fatalities, the combined values do not correspond linearly to those reported in the individual data sources. Appendix A shows how we combined the data sets and explains where we used additional analysis to complete some categories.

Types of Injuries and Fatalities for All Services

Although occupational injury and fatality rates are significantly elevated for both firefighters and police, the types and causes of injury and death for the two groups are quite different. Stress, becoming lost or trapped, and vehicle accidents are the primary causes of death for firefighters, whereas police deaths are due almost exclusively to vehicle accidents and assaults (Figure 4.2). The vast majority of EMS line-of-duty deaths are due to vehicle accidents and accidents involving rescue helicopters.

---

[5] NFPA (1995–2000b).

[6] Weighting the state injury rates by both responder population in the state (from NPSIB 2002b) and state population (from the 2000 Census), the incidence rate for employees of local government police agencies was about 17.5 per 100 full time workers. Because this number includes non-emergency response personnel, the rate for responders may be even higher.

[7] Because the injury counts for firefighters and police are reported from different sources, the requirements for defining an injury event in the NFPA and SOII databases may be different.

[8] Maguire et al. (2002) estimate the fatality rate for EMS personnel at 12.7 per 100,000 workers, compared with 5.0 for all occupations.

34

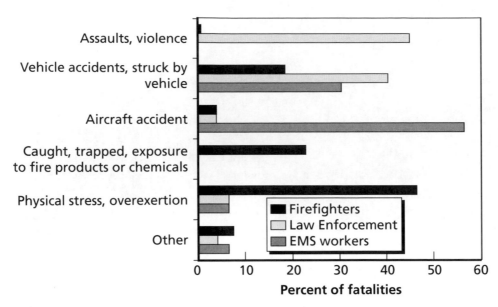

Percent of fatalities

SOURCE: NFPA (1995–2000a), National Law Enforcement Officers Memorial Fund (2002a), and National EMS Memorial Service (2002).
NOTE: Data are for 1995–2000 for firefighters, 1992–2001 for police, and 1998–2001 for EMS.

RAND *TR100-4.2*

Figure 4.2—Cause of Fatal Injuries for Firefighters, Police, and EMS Workers

The nature and body parts involved in line-of-duty injuries experienced by emergency responders also vary among the three services, according to an analysis of information collected in the NEISS database (Figure 4.3). Although the overall breakdown of injuries is similar, the services differ because each service faces a different combination of emergency duties and associated hazards.

NEISS data are collected from emergency room records and therefore represent a more severe sample of injuries than those covered by other sources elsewhere in this report (by comparison, in almost half of the firefighter injuries included in the NFIRS database for 1998, the injured firefighter was not transported to a medical care facility). Unlike individual responder-specific data sources, which may have different inclusion and coding criteria, NEISS applies identical standards to data on members of all three emergency response services. Therefore, NEISS data are particularly useful for comparing injuries experienced by different types of emergency responders. (The NEISS data reported here are preliminary and should not be further cited.)

Percent of Injuries within Occupations

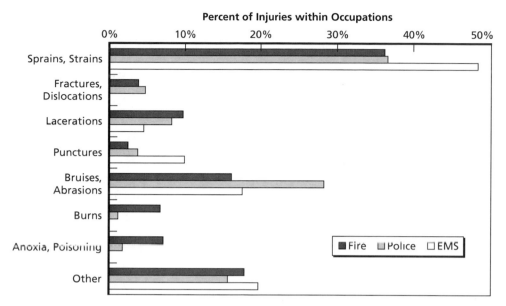

SOURCE: L. L. Jackson, NIOSH, unpublished data.

[a]These estimates represent preliminary data and should not be cited or quoted.

RAND *TR100-4.3*

Figure 4.3—Nature of Injury for Firefighters, Police, and EMS Injuries, 1996–1998, Based on National Estimates[a]

According to the NEISS data, the most common occupational injuries experienced by firefighters are sprains and strains, which account for about 36 percent of all injuries.[9] Fractures and dislocations make up about 4 percent of injuries, and cuts and bruises (bruises, abrasions, lacerations, and punctures) make up 28 percent. These injuries are similar to those for the other services, indicating that all emergency responders may share the hazards that cause these traumatic injuries. Burns and asphyxiation each account for about 7 percent of firefighter injuries. The prevalence of these two types of injuries (compared with those for other emergency responders) is consistent with an increased risk of exposure to heat, smoke, and other fire products and hazardous substances.

About 37 percent of police injuries are sprains or strains; 5 percent are fractures or dislocations; and 40 percent are cuts and bruises, including 28 percent that are bruises or abrasions. The significantly increased incidence of bruises and abrasions is consistent with an increased risk of assault or violence against law enforcement responders.

---

[9] Firearms-related injuries were excluded, but firearms were involved—not necessarily *used*—in only 3 percent of nonfatal assaults on police officers in 2000, accounting for only 1.3 percent of injuries resulting from assault, so this exclusion amounts to less than 1 percent of all police injuries. See Federal Bureau of Investigation (2002).

The NEISS probability-based sample of 67 hospital emergency departments contains treatment information for about 600 EMS, 2,000 firefighter, and 3,000 police injuries. These cases were used to extrapolate to national estimates of injuries treated in U.S. hospital emergency departments. However, the small number of EMS injury cases precludes reliable reporting of national estimates for some injury subcategories compared with those for firefighters and police. Nearly half of EMS injuries are sprains and strains, and 32 percent are cuts or bruises. The distribution of cuts and bruises among EMS workers is different than in the other services: Among police and firefighters, lacerations are two to four times as common as punctures. For EMS responders, this is reversed, indicating an increased risk of injury from needles or other "sharps." Such injuries are the primary mechanism of infectious disease exposure for these responders.

Because the NEISS database includes more detailed information on the site of injury, the NEISS data can also be used to describe how responder injuries are distributed among different parts of the body. Although the distribution of most injuries is similar among the three services, EMS responders suffer a much larger percentage of lower trunk injuries than do police and firefighters and a smaller percentage of injuries to the lower extremities.[10]

Firefighter Injuries and Fatalities

The firefighter injury and fatality data can be broken out by cause of injury, nature of injury, and activity and type of duty, including some information on the severity of nonfatal injuries.

Nature of Injury

Nearly half of all firefighter fatalities are "cardiac" in nature (Table 4.2). Most of these are heart attacks. Thirty percent of fatalities are traumatic injuries, most of which are vehicle-related (accidents and struck by vehicle). Another 19 percent are due to burns, asphyxiation, or other respiratory distress, usually occurring when a firefighter is trapped in a burning building. About 5 percent of deaths are caused by all other natures of injury.

The breakdown of injuries is significantly different. Cardiac injuries comprise only 1 percent of the total, but these injuries are much more likely to be severe than other types of injury. Severity was calculated by the percentage of injuries

---

[10] L. L. Jackson, NIOSH, unpublished data.

Table 4.2
Average Annual Counts of Firefighter Injuries and Fatalities, 1995–2000

Nature of Injury	Minor	Moderate	Severe	Fatality
Sprains, strains	25,600	15,700	500[a]	29[a]
Fractures, dislocations	500	1,400		
Cuts, bruises	11,100	4,200	100	0
Eye injuries	2,700	700	0	0
Burns	3,000	1,800	100	5
Asphyxiation, hazmat inhalation, drowning, other respiratory	2,500	2,500	400	14
Thermal stress	1,700	1,200	300	0
Cardiac	200	600	400	45
All other types	7,300	3,400	300	5
Total	54,500	31,400	2,000	97

SOURCES: Fatalities from NFPA (1995–2000a) and U.S. Fire Administration (1996–2001). The values reported are the average of the two sources. Total injury counts from NFPA (1995–2000b).

NOTES: Totals may not add due to rounding. Injuries were sorted into minor, moderate, and severe using percentages calculated from the NFIRS 1998 firefighter casualty module. Because the NFIRS database contains a different sample of injuries (about 95 percent fireground) than the NFPA injury reports (about 50 percent fireground), injury breakdowns by severity should be considered approximate and are rounded to the nearest hundred.

[a]For sprains, strains and fractures, dislocations, values are combined for severe and fatal injuries because distinctions between these natures are often not meaningful for more severe injuries.

that are identified as minor, moderate, and severe or worse in the NFIRS 1998 database.[11]

NFIRS defines a *severe injury* as one in which "the situation is potentially life threatening if the condition remains uncontrolled. Immediate medical care is necessary even though body processes may still be functioning and vital signs may be normal." A *moderate injury* is defined as one in which "there is little danger of death or permanent disability. Quick medical care is advisable. This category includes injuries such as fractures or lacerations requiring sutures." A *minor injury* is defined as one in which "the patient is not in danger of death or permanent disability. Immediate medical care is not necessary."[12]

More than one-third of cardiac injuries are severe or worse, and half are moderate. Asphyxiation and other respiratory injuries (about 6 percent of all injuries), thermal stress (about 6 percent), and fractures and dislocations (about 2 percent) are also among the more severe types of injury. For each type, 6 to 9 percent of injuries are severe or worse. Together, these four natures account for more than one-half of severe injuries and fatalities but less than 10 percent of minor injuries.

All other natures of injury make up 87 percent of injuries but are less severe than fractures; dislocations; and cardiac, respiratory, and heat stress injuries. Non-fracture traumatic injuries, such as sprains and strains (47 percent of all on-duty injuries) and burns (6 percent of injuries), tend to be somewhat less severe (about 60 percent are minor injuries, and about 1 to 1.5 percent are severe or worse) and account for a smaller fraction of severe injuries and deaths than of minor and moderate injuries. Cuts and bruises (17 percent of injuries) and eye injuries (4 percent of injuries) are common but are nearly always minor. From 1995 to 2001, only one firefighter death was classified as a cut-type injury.

A comparison of the NFPA and IAFF survey data for all on-duty injuries shows that the types of injuries suffered by volunteer and career firefighters are very similar. There is some evidence from these sources that volunteer firefighters suffer more eye injuries, cuts and bruises, and fractures or dislocations and fewer

---

[11] NFIRS uses a 6-point severity scale. Minor injuries are coded as 1, moderate injuries are coded as 2, severe injuries as 3, life-threatening as 4, and codes 5 and 6 refer to fatalities. "Severe or worse injuries" refers to codes 3 and 4.

[12] This is a life-safety definition of severity, but that is not the only way to consider severity. For example, the person affected may consider a burn to the arms or face that causes scarring but no other long-term effects substantially worse than a broken arm because of the social and emotional impact of the scarring, even though NFIRS might report both as "moderate."

cardiac-related injuries. However, these differences are small and may be artifacts resulting from differences in data collection by the two organizations.

Type of Duty and Activity

Just over half of firefighter injuries (51 percent) and two-fifths of fatalities (44 percent) occur on the fireground, with the remainder being distributed among responding to and returning from calls, nonfire emergencies such as EMS calls, training, and other on-duty events (see Figure 4.4).

Although the percentages of firefighter injuries and fatalities occurring during most types of duty were similar, the percentage of deaths that occur while en route to or returning from an alarm is much higher than the corresponding percentage of injuries. Only 6 percent of injuries occurred while responding to or returning from calls, but this activity accounted for approximately one-fourth of all fatalities (frequently as a result of motor vehicle accidents). Nonfire emergencies, primarily EMS calls, were responsible for 16 percent of injuries and 11 percent of fatalities.

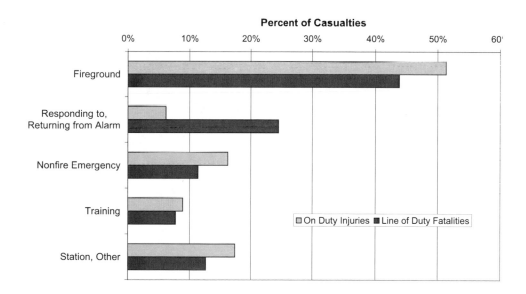

SOURCES: Fatalities from NFPA (1995–2000a) and U.S. Fire Administration (2002). Injuries from NFPA (1995–2000b) and International Association of Fire Fighters (1993–1998).
NOTE: The values shown are the average of the two sources.

Figure 4.4—Type of Duty for Firefighter Injuries and Fatalities

The large number of injuries and fatalities that occur at the fireground is also striking given the comparatively small amount of time firefighters are involved in fireground operations. In 2000, fire incidents represented only 8 percent of the calls for service performed by fire departments. In contrast, medical responses made up 60 percent of service calls.[13]

Information about types of activity firefighters were involved in at the time of injury is available only for fireground injuries and fatalities. About half of fireground injuries and fatalities occur while firefighters are participating in fire attack, more than in any other activity (Figure 4.5).

Burn, respiratory, and thermal stress injuries make up a higher percentage of injuries on the fireground than during other types of duty, whereas other types of injuries are similar or somewhat less frequent during fireground operations. The high percentage of injuries occurring during fire attack probably results not only from the danger involved in the activity but also from the fact that fire attack—in which many personnel are involved for significant periods of time—is a part of nearly every firefighting operation. About 4 percent of injuries and 13 percent of fatalities occur during search and rescue operations, and about 3 percent of injuries and 13 percent of fatalities happen while establishing water supply. Search and rescue often involves entering a burning building without a hoseline because the lives of the occupants may be at risk, and the hazards, for the most part, are similar to fire attack. The disproportionately high number of fatalities indicates especially high level risks associated with search and rescue operations. The fatalities occurring during water supply operations are primarily due to heart attacks. Water supply is one of the first tasks performed on the scene, so this may be the first physically stressful task performed by a firefighter arriving at an incident.

Ventilation and forcible entry operations account for 10 percent of injuries and 5 percent of fatalities; salvage and overhaul accounts for more than 15 percent of injuries but only 1.5 percent of fatalities. Although significant injury hazards are involved in ventilation, forcible entry, salvage, and overhaul, the potential for the highest-level risk during these activities is lower than it is for more "forward" activities, such as fire attack or search and rescue. In addition, salvage and overhaul operations tend to occur in a calmer, more controlled environment after much or all of the fire has been extinguished.

---

[13] An additional 4 percent of calls were categorized as "mutual aid." This may include additional fire incident responses. See NFPA (2002).

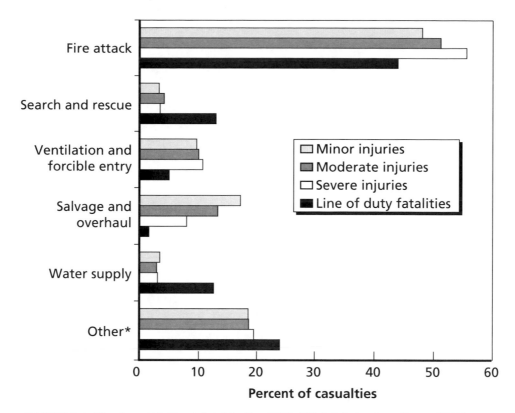

SOURCE: Fatalities from U.S. Fire Administration (1996–2001). Injuries from Karter (2000), adjusted by analysis of the NFIRS 1998 firefighter casualty module.

NOTES: The NFIRS 1998 data were used to estimate the incidence of activities unreported in Karter (2000) and to reclassify certain natures based on additional information contained in the NFIRS database. Injuries were sorted into minor, moderate, and severe using percentages calculated from the NFIRS 1998 firefighter casualty module for fireground injuries. Severe injuries are based on a sample of fewer than 200 injuries, and therefore there is significant uncertainty involved in calculating both the breakdown of severe injuries by activity and the percentage of severe injuries occurring during each activity. Investigation of the NFIRS 1998 data indicates that many of the injuries in the "other" category occurred while picking up or carrying tools on the fireground.

RAND *TR100-4.5*

Figure 4.5—Firefighter Activity for Fireground Injuries and Fatalities

Cause of Injury

There are four main causes of firefighter injuries and fatalities on the fireground, each accounting for about 22 to 25 percent of the total: being struck by or making contact with objects; falling or jumping; exposure to fire products, chemicals, or extreme weather; and physical stress or overexertion (see Figure 4.6).

Physical stress or overexertion and exposure are the most severe of the main causes of injury. For each cause, 4 to 5 percent of fireground injuries are

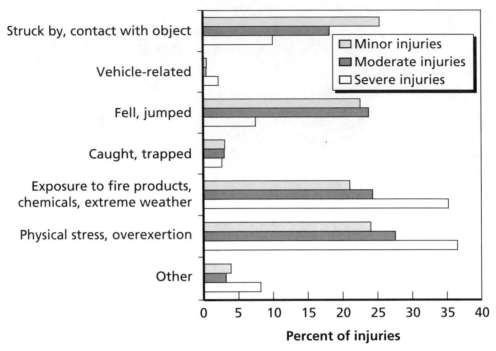

SOURCE: NFPA (1995–2000b) and Karter (2000), adjusted using NFIRS 1998 data.

NOTES: The NFIRS 1998 data were used to estimate the incidence of activities unreported in Karter (2000) and to reclassify certain natures based on additional information contained in the NFIRS database. The values reported are the average of the two sources. Injuries were sorted into minor, moderate, and severe using percentages calculated from the NFIRS 1998 firefighter casualty module for fireground injuries. Severe injuries are based on a sample of fewer than 200 injuries and therefore there is significant uncertainty involved in calculating both the breakdown of severe injuries by activity and the percentage of severe injuries occurring during each activity

RAND *TR100-4.6*

Figure 4.6—Firefighter Fireground Injuries by Cause

severe or worse, and more than 40 percent are moderate or worse. As can be seen in Figures 4.2 and 4.6, about two-thirds of severe fireground injuries and one-half of fatalities[14] are caused by either exposure or physical stress/overexertion.

Less than 2 percent of fireground injuries caused by falls or by being struck or making contact with an object are severe or worse, and less than 40 percent are moderate or worse. Together, these causes account for nearly as many minor and moderate injuries as physical stress/overexertion and exposure, but only one-sixth of severe injuries. Vehicle accidents, a subset of being struck by or making

---

[14] In nonfatal instances of exposure to fire products, the firefighter escapes to a safe area or is rescued, and the cause of injury is typically classified as exposure. If the firefighter is trapped and unable to escape, and dies from asphyxiation or burns, the cause of death is typically classified as caught/trapped, even though the nature and mechanism of injury are the same in both cases. Combining caught/trapped with exposure, about 70 percent of line-of-duty fatalities are caused by either exposure or physical stress and overexertion.

contact with an object, account for less than 1 percent of fireground injuries[15] but 18 percent of fatalities (22 percent if aircraft accidents are included). Nonfatal injuries occurring in vehicle accidents tend to be more severe than with most other causes.

Occupational Injury and Illness Retirements

The incident- and survey-based data above provide a good description of acute injury events. Although some acute injury events, such as cardiac injuries, are frequently indicative of long-term conditions, most are sudden events in which the measurable consequences are immediately apparent.

One source of information on long-term injury and illness is data describing firefighter retirements resulting from occupational injury or illness. Often, retirements are due to conditions that build up slowly and at some point become too debilitating for the responder to continue working. They can be described by nature and body part but not by event or activity. Breakdowns by event or activity are not relevant for conditions that develop over long periods; in many cases, the injury or illness cannot be definitively linked to a particular event or incident.[16]

From 1993 to 1998, occupational injury and illness requirements made up about 27 percent of all firefighter retirements (Figure 4.7). Occupational injury retirements (chiefly back, limb, and torso pain) are about twice as common as illness retirements (primarily heart and lung disease and cancer). Of the 27 percent of all retirements that are injury related (about 1,500 each year), about one-third are due to back injury. Other injury types—including limb, torso, hand, foot, and face injuries—together account for one-third of occupational injury retirements. The final third of injury retirements are due to occupational illness, including heart disease, lung disease, cancer, hearing loss, mental stress, and other causes.

---

[15] The data on cause of injury include only fireground injuries. It is likely that injuries occurring in other types of duty (especially responding to and returning from alarms) would result in vehicle accidents accounting for a greater share of all on-duty injuries than fireground injuries.

[16] The available data do not contain information on cause, event, or type of activity for any occupational injury retirements.

44

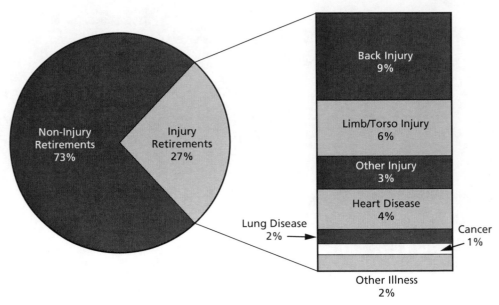

SOURCE: International Association of Fire Fighters (1993–1998).
RAND TR100-4.7

Figure 4.7—Breakdown of Firefighter Occupational Injury Retirements

Injury Incidence Matrix

The injury incidence matrix shown in Figure 4.8 summarizes the data discussed in the previous sections to show graphically during which combinations of activities and hazards firefighters are most often injured, as well as the injuries that are most likely to result from each combination. Minor injuries are not included in the matrix, both because more-severe injuries are of greater concern and because adopting this convention facilitates comparison with the data available for law enforcement responders.[17] Black cells correspond to combinations of activities and hazards with the most injuries, dark gray to high incidence, light gray to moderate incidence, and white to low incidence. Within each cell, the most common types of injury are listed, with those most frequently encountered listed first.

The incidence matrix was created by classifying all injuries reported in the NFIRS 1998 firefighter casualty module that were of at least moderate severity and occurred on the fireground by cause of injury and activity (only the highest-

---

[17] Law enforcement data are drawn from the BLS Survey of Occupational Injuries and Illnesses, which only includes injuries that result in lost workdays.

Cause of Injury

Firefighter Injuries	Fell, jumped	Caught, trapped	Struck by or contact with object	Exposure to fire products	Exposure to chemicals	Physical stress, over-exertion
Fire attack, search and rescue	Trauma Cuts/bruises	Burns Trauma	Cuts/bruises Trauma Burns	Burns Respiratory Heat stress	Respiratory	Trauma Heat stress Cardiac Respiratory
Ventilation and forcible entry	Trauma		Cuts/bruises Trauma	Respiratory Heat stress		Trauma Heat stress
Salvage and overhaul	Trauma		Cuts/bruises Trauma			Trauma Heat stress Cardiac
Incident scene support activities	Trauma Cuts/bruises		Cuts/bruises			Trauma Heat stress Cardiac
Riding on or driving apparatus	Trauma		Trauma Cuts/bruises Burns			Trauma

Fireground activity (vertical axis label)

Legend:
- ■ Highest incidence
- ▨ High incidence
- ▢ Moderate incidence
- □ Low incidence

SOURCE: Based on data from the NFIRS 1998 Firefighter Casualty Module.

NOTES: Black cells indicate at least 150 reported injuries (10 percent of the total); dark-gray cells 36 to 66 injuries (2 to 4 percent); and light-gray cells 15 to 28 injuries (1 to 2 percent). Injuries with cause or activity unreported or reported as "other" are not included. Because of sample size, differences between some dark-gray and light-gray and some light-gray and white cells may not be statistically significant. Incident scene support activities include water supply operations and picking up and moving tools.

RAND *TR100-4.8*

Figure 4.8—Injury Incidence Matrix for Moderate and Severe Firefighter Fireground Injuries by Cause and Activity

frequency hazards and activities are shown). Vehicle-related injuries are more frequent than indicated in the matrix, as injuries that occur while responding to or returning from an incident are not included.

The highest number of injuries from all causes occurs during fire attack and search and rescue. Fire attack is not only one of the most dangerous fireground activities but also one of the most common. As a result, the high numbers of injuries are related both to the level of hazard and to the time firefighters are exposed while involved in the activity. Of the fire attack-cause combinations, the highest-risk combinations are exposure to fire products and from physical stress or overexertion, each accounting for almost 20 percent of moderate and severe fireground injuries.

In activities other than fire attack, firefighters are injured most frequently from falls during salvage and overhaul, incident scene support activities, or from apparatus; and physical stress and overexertion or being struck by or making contact with an object during ventilation, forcible entry, salvage and overhaul, and incident scene support activities.

Police Injuries and Fatalities

Police injury data allow breakdowns by cause of injury, as well as by nature of nonfatal injuries. However, because of the inclusion criteria of the BLS SOII database, these breakdowns are available only for lost-work-time injuries. In comparison with the firefighter data, this means that many less-severe injuries (including most that would be classified "minor" and some that would be classified "moderate" in NFIRS) are not included.

Almost 90 percent of police line-of-duty fatalities are either assault- or vehicle-related (Figure 4.9). Most of the remainder are heart attacks brought on by physical stress. Assaults (27 percent) and vehicle accidents (16 percent) together make up nearly half of lost-time injuries. The other most common causes of lost-time injury are falls (19 percent), and physical stress or overexertion (25 percent). While almost all homicides are shootings (more than 90 percent), more than 80 percent of assailants in nonfatal attacks between 1991 and 2000 used "personal weapons" such as hands and feet.[18]

The severity measure used by the Bureau of Labor Statistics is median days away from work for all lost-work-time injuries of each type. We combined these data across three years and occasionally across multiple categories of cause of injury. The resulting severity information for these categories of injury is shown for each

---

[18] Information on assaults from Federal Bureau of Investigation (2002).

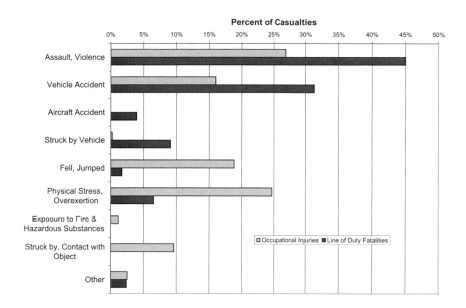

SOURCE: Fatalities from National Law Enforcement Officers Memorial Fund (2002a). Injuries from Survey of Occupational Injuries and Illnesses, Bureau of Labor Statistics (2003b).

NOTES: Data include police and detectives (occupation code 418), State of New York, at the local government level, for the years 1998–2000. "Struck by vehicle" refers to officers struck while not inside a vehicle.

Figure 4.9   Cause of Injury for Police Lost-Work-Time Injuries and Fatalities

cause in Figure 4.10.[19] Although this measure of severity is significantly different than the judgment-based scale used in NFIRS, it does provide a way to compare severity across injury types.

Of the most common causes of injury, falls and physical stress had a severity of five days away from work, and assaults and vehicle accidents, four days. Exposure to fire and hazardous substances (corresponding to BLS categories "temperature extremes" and "caustic, noxious, or allergenic substances") was responsible for about 1 percent of lost-time injuries, with a severity of four days away from work.

---

[19] BLS is able to calculate the median days away from work for each category for each data year. The severity figure above, for three years of data, was calculated in two ways: (1) the median value of the reported severity for every category regardless of the number of injuries, rounded to the nearest whole number, and (2) the weighted average of the median value for each category, rounded to the nearest whole number. In all cases, these methods produced the same value.

48

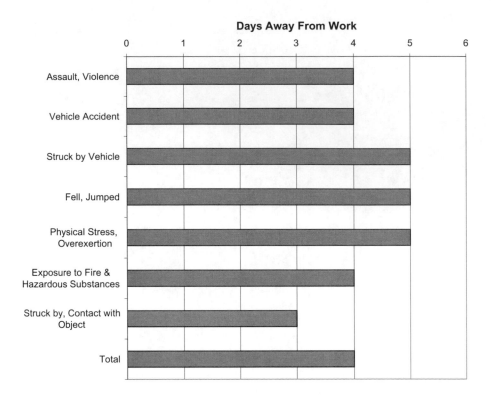

SOURCE: Survey of Occupational Injuries and Illnesses, Bureau of Labor Statistics (2003b).
NOTES: Data include police and detectives (occupation code 418), State of New York, at the local government level, for the years 1998–2000. "Struck by vehicle" refers to officers struck while not inside a vehicle.

Figure 4.10—Severity of Police Lost-Work-Time Injuries, by Cause of Injury

Injury Incidence Matrix

Although data on activity at the time of injury are not available for police, a single dimension injury incidence matrix (Figure 4.11) can be constructed for police using data from the BLS Survey of Occupational Injuries and Illnesses, similar to Figure 4.8. The data used are for police and detectives employed by local governments in New York State for 1998 through 2000. Only the highest-frequency causes of injury are shown.

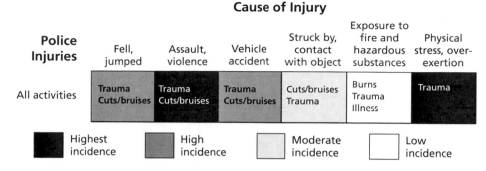

SOURCE: Based on data from the Survey of Occupational Injuries and Illnesses, Bureau of Labor Statistics (2003b).

NOTES: Data are for police and detectives, State of New York, at the local government level, for the years 1998–2000. Black cells represent at least 5,000 injuries; dark-gray cells at least 4,000 injuries; and the light-gray cell about 2,400 injuries. SOII estimates a total of 25,000 injuries for 1998–2000; the estimate in the figure is based on a smaller number of recorded cases.

RAND TR100-4.11

Figure 4.11—Injury Incidence Matrix for Police Lost-Work-Time Injuries by Cause

As with the firefighter injury incidence matrix, black cells represent hazards resulting in the most injuries, dark gray cells represent high incidence, and the light gray cell, moderate incidence. Police are most often injured in falls, assaults, vehicle-related accidents, and through stress or overexertion. From all causes, the most common types of injury are traumatic injuries, such as sprains and strains, and cuts and bruises. Police are also at risk of burns and symptoms of illness as a result of exposure to fire and hazardous substances (in the figure, "illness" indicates injury cases where symptoms are present from a disease or illness but where a definite diagnosis is lacking or is unclassifiable). These exposure-related injuries represent less than 1 percent of all law enforcement injuries.

EMS Injuries and Fatalities

Data on EMS responder injuries and fatalities are limited. A recently published analysis of EMS line-of-duty fatalities using data from the Census of Fatal Occupational Injuries and NEMSMS data estimated an average of 19 EMS responder deaths per year from 1992 to 1997.[20] The information available on causes of fatalities indicates that emergency medical responders are most often killed in aircraft and motor vehicle accidents (Figure 4.12). From 1998 through 2001, over one–half (56 percent) of the 46 line-of-duty fatalities reported to the

_____

[20] In this analysis, motor vehicle accidents were the leading cause of death, followed by aircraft accidents (Maguire et al., 2002).

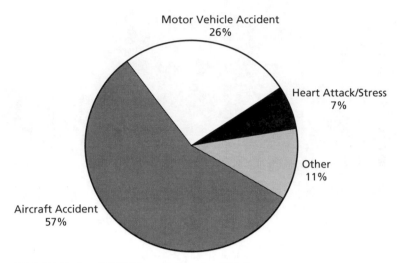

Motor Vehicle Accident
26%

Heart Attack/Stress
7%

Other
11%

Aircraft Accident
57%

SOURCE: National EMS Memorial Service (2002).
RAND *TR100-4.12*

Figure 4.12—Cause of Injury for EMS Line-of-Duty Fatalities, 1998–2001

National EMS Memorial Service were due to rescue helicopter crashes, and another 25 percent were due to motor vehicle accidents.[21] Other causes of death include drowning (2 percent), being struck by vehicles while on foot (4 percent), and heart attacks or other physical stress (7 percent).

Other than the fatality data in Figure 4.12 and the NEISS data included in Figure 4.3, the only data sources for injuries to EMS workers focus on infectious disease exposures. Among emergency responders, emergency medical personnel have the highest risk of exposure to infectious disease: From 1996 to 1998, 85 percent of exposures reported by firefighters occurred when performing EMS duties, compared with only about 10 percent on the fireground.[22]

The most common exposures in 1993–1998 (an exposure does not necessarily mean that the responder was infected) were to tuberculosis (about 32 percent of exposures), HIV/AIDS (about 18 percent), meningitis (about 11 percent), and hepatitis A, B, and C (about 12 percent together).[23] At least one police officer has died of AIDS complications after being assaulted by a suspect with an HIV-infected needle.[24]

---

[21] This number does not include six deaths also recorded by the U. S. Fire Administration as firefighter fatalities.

[22] International Association of Fire Fighters (1996–1998).

[23] International Association of Fire Fighters (1993–1998).

[24] National Law Enforcement Officers Memorial Fund (2002a).

Emergency responders are exposed to diseases through a variety of mechanisms. Blood-borne pathogens are of the greatest concern. According to a surveillance of hospital-based emergency medical technicians, 65 of 354 (18 percent) EMTs for whom records are available reported exposure to bodily fluids between June 1995 and February 11, 2002, with four being exposed more than once.[25] About half of the exposures were due to percutaneous injuries such as needle sticks, while the other half were due mostly to skin and mucous membrane exposures. Six of the EMTs were tested for tuberculosis after respiratory exposure (none was infected), while six other EMTs tested positive for tuberculosis during routine testing.

Findings

Significant data are available to describe line-of-duty injuries and fatalities experienced by firefighters and police officers, and some data are available to describe hazards faced by EMS personnel as well. The available data indicate some similarity across the services in the risks faced by emergency responders, but also significant differences.

The main similarities are (1) many deaths occur as a result of vehicle accidents, and (2) the most common natures of injury experienced by each type of responder are cuts and bruises, sprains, strains, and other trauma. For all three services, a significant portion of injuries and fatalities occur away from the incident scene. Only half of firefighter injuries occur on the scene of fire emergencies, and less than half of fatalities. For police and EMS, breakdowns by type of duty are not available. However, the high prevalence of deaths and injuries resulting from vehicle accidents in these professions strongly suggests that responding to and returning from incidents are also very hazardous in these services.

The differences in occupational hazards among services are related to the specialized tasks that each performs. In addition to cuts and other trauma such as sprains and strains, the types of injury most experienced by firefighters are burns, asphyxiation and other respiratory injuries, and thermal stress. Physical stress and overexertion, falls, being struck by or making contact with objects, and exposure to fire products are the primary causes of injury at the fire scene. Physical stress, becoming lost or trapped in a fire situation, and vehicle accidents are the primary causes of death. Physical stress is responsible for nearly half of all on-duty deaths.

---

[25] National Center for Infectious Diseases (2002).

Most injuries to police are traumatic injuries resulting from vehicle accidents, falls, assaults, or physical stress. Nine out of ten line-of-duty deaths are due to vehicle accidents or assaults. Most of the remainder are due to being struck by a vehicle and stress or overexertion.

The information about EMS injuries and hazards is scarce and far less definitive. EMS personnel are most at risk of sprains and strains, and they have a much higher proportion of back injuries than other responders do. EMS personnel also have a high risk of infectious disease exposure, mostly through percutaneous injuries such as needle sticks. Nearly all on-duty deaths on which data are available are due to aircraft and vehicle accidents.

5. Conclusions

The emergency response community represents a significant population of workers exposed to a particularly intense and variable hazard environment in the course of their work activities. The approximately 1,100,000 firefighters, 600,000 patrol and investigative law enforcement officers, and 500,000 emergency medical service responders answer calls for assistance and service that result in significant numbers of occupational injuries and fatalities. The review presented in this document has shown that extensive surveillance data are available to describe the injuries and fatalities suffered by firefighters. A lesser, but still useful, amount of information is available for police casualties. Emergency medical services data are scarce, and few conclusions can be drawn from the existing data. This document represents a collection and synthesis of currently available data.

Although current data sources have significant limitations in addressing portions of the emergency response community (particularly EMS responders), ongoing changes to the occupation coding of federal government data sources will make it easier to examine injuries to law enforcement and EMS responders. One of the primary surveillance data sources, the Survey of Occupational Injuries and Illnesses, will switch to a new occupation coding for the 2003 data year, and data are expected to become available in 2005. Data sources such as the Survey of Occupational Injuries and Illnesses and the National Fire Incident Reporting System enable detailed examination of responder protection needs and strategies for providing that protection.

The results presented in this report provide an integrated view of what is known about the numbers and characteristics of responder injuries and fatalities. Many of the results are not surprising, such as the seriousness of the assault and vehicle-related hazards to police and the significant heat and physical stress risks faced by firefighters. However, some of the findings—most notably, the fact that falls and physical stress and overexertion result in nearly as many police injuries as assaults and vehicle accidents do and are relatively more severe—are unexpected.

Overall, physical stress and overexertion, becoming lost or trapped, and vehicle accidents are the primary causes of death for firefighters. Physical stress and overexertion, falls, being struck by or making contact with objects, and exposure to fire products are the primary causes of injury at the fire scene. For law enforcement officers, deaths are due almost exclusively to vehicle accidents and assaults. Police are most at risk of traumatic injuries resulting from vehicle accidents, falls, assaults, and physical stress. The limited available data indicate that EMS personnel are most at risk of sprains and strains, especially back injuries, and also have a significantly increased risk of infectious disease exposure, mostly through percutaneous injuries such as needle sticks. The majority of recent line-of-duty EMS deaths resulted from motor vehicle and rescue helicopter accidents.

The surveillance data clearly show that certain hazards are common to all responders: the risk of vehicle-related deaths, traumatic injuries such as sprains and strains, and cuts and bruises. At the same time, the data highlight the particular hazards associated with each service: burns, thermal stress, asphyxiation and other respiratory injuries for firefighters; falls, assaults, and physical stress for police; and back injuries and infectious disease exposure for emergency medical responders. By identifying combinations of activities and hazards that currently result in the largest number and most serious responder injuries, these data provide an important input for setting protective technology development and program priorities. The data can provide a route for identifying combinations of nature and cause of injury, body part involved, and responder activity where injury reduction efforts might be most effectively applied. Such detailed analyses are most accessible for firefighters because of the comparative richness of the relevant data sources.

However, injury counts alone are not sufficient to fully define the protection needs of emergency responders. By definition, they measure the negative consequences of exposure to particular risks over particular time periods. As a result, surveillance data give a preferential focus to "routine" activities because those tasks occupy the vast majority of responders' time. Therefore, the levels of injury should not be interpreted as direct measures of the level of risk faced by responders for *all* activities. Activities performed by responders for short periods of time, or events that occur infrequently, may involve levels of risk much higher than more-common tasks. Events such as major disasters, structural collapse, civil disturbance, bomb disposal, hostage situations, and terrorism response involve intense hazards not normally encountered in routine activities. As a result, they may be of much greater concern than the everyday events that produce the majority of injuries and fatalities. The opposite is also sometimes true: Certain catastrophic events , such as the collapse of the World Trade Center towers, are frequently excluded (with cause) from data sources as outliers. And the consequences of other potential hazards that have not yet been realized, such as large-scale terrorist attacks involving biological or chemical weapons, cannot be effectively captured. To fully assess responders' personal protection needs, all high-risk nonroutine activities must be considered separately from routine activities, whether they dominate the injury and fatality surveillance data or are lost within it.

Similarly, while direct counts of injuries and the severity measures discussed in this report are excellent indicators of the scope of a health and safety problem, they cannot completely capture all the issues associated with the problem. For instance, although sprains and strains are the most common injuries experienced by responders in all three services, responders typically do not view them as a primary concern. Thus, merely using injury frequencies when setting priorities for protective technology will not adequately address the concerns of the community.

To address both the limitations of a purely data-based approach to this area, RAND has also gathered information directly from the emergency response community through an extensive structured interview process. The results of that effort, included in a separate report (LaTourrette et al., 2003), are a critical complement to the surveillance data presented here.

In addition to demonstrating the utility of the currently available data and data sources, this analysis also suggests a range of potential future efforts that could contribute to a better understanding of emergency responder injuries and fatalities and the effects of personal protective technology. The diversity of data sources on emergency responders suggests that efforts to interconnect information from different databases could be valuable. An area of particular potential is fatality data—where the comparatively small number of cases and the availability of rich narrative information could enable many types of analysis. High-resolution injury sources, such as the NFIRS database and to a lesser extent the BLS Survey of Occupational Injuries and Illnesses, could be sampled to explore specific relationships between the nature and circumstance of injuries. Furthermore, efforts to aggregate injury data for police and EMS workers to increase sample size, obtain information on responder activity at the time of their injury, and further support studies of long-term health outcomes could provide additional insight. Such interconnection and analysis efforts can help formulate and answer detailed questions about protective technology design and performance in specific response situations.

References

Beaumont, James J., George S. T. Chu, Jeffrey R. Jones, Marc B. Schenker, James A. Singleton, Lillian G. Piantanida, and Marc Reiterman, "An Epidemiologic Study of Cancer and Other Causes of Mortality in San Francisco Firefighters," *American Journal of Industrial Medicine*, Vol. 19, 1991, pp. 357–372.

Bureau of Labor Statistics, U.S. Department of Labor, Survey of Occupational Injuries and Illnesses, http://www.bls.gov/iif/oshstate.htm, accessed October 31, 2002.

Bureau of Labor Statistics, U.S. Department of Labor, Occupational Employment Statistics Survey by Occupation, 2001, http://www.bls.gov/oes/2001/oes_29He.htm, accessed March 10, 2003a.

Bureau of Labor Statistics, U.S. Department of Labor, Survey of Occupational Injuries and Illnesses, database report. Obtained via personal communication from Boston-NY Regional Office, March 2003b.

CDC, *see* Centers for Disease Control and Prevention

Centers for Disease Control and Prevention, U.S. Department of Health and Human Services, "Public Health Consequences Among First Responders to Emergency Events Associated With Illicit Methamphetamine Laboratories—Selected States, 1996–1999," *Morbidity and Mortality Weekly Report*, Vol. 49, No. 45, November 17, 2000, pp. 1021–1024.

Clarke, Cindy, and Mark J. Zak, "Fatalities to Law Enforcement Officers and Firefighters, 1992–1997," *Compensation and Working Conditions*, Summer 1999, pp. 3–7.

Demers, Paul A., Harvey Checkoway, Thomas L. Vaughn, Noel S. Weiss, Nicholas J. Heyer, and Linda Rosenstock, "Cancer Incidence Among Firefighters in Seattle and Tacoma, Washington (United States)," *Cancer Causes and Control*, Vol. 5, 1994, pp. 129–135.

Demers, Paul A., Nicholas J. Heyer, and Linda Rosenstock, "Mortality Among Firefighters from Three Northwestern United States Cities," *British Journal of Industrial Medicine*, Vol. 49, 1992, pp. 664–670.

EMS Magazine, "State & Province Survey, 2001," http://www.emsmagazine.com/SURVEY/index.html, accessed October 15, 2002.

Federal Bureau of Investigation, *Law Enforcement Officers Killed and Assaulted 2000*, available at http://www.fbi.gov/ucr/killed/00leoka.pdf, accessed October 31, 2002.

Feuer, Elizabeth, and Kenneth Rosenman, "Mortality in Police and Firefighters in New Jersey," *American Journal of Industrial Medicine*, Vol. 9, 1986, pp. 517–527.

Guidotti, Tee L., "Occupational Mortality Among Firefighters: Assessing the Association," *Journal of Occupational and Environmental Medicine*, Vol. 37, No. 12, December 1995, pp. 1348–1355.

Haddon, Jr., W., "Advances in the Epidemiology of Injuries as a Basis for Public Policy," *Public Health Reports*, Vol. 95, No. 5, 1980, pp. 411–421.

Hall, Jr., John R., and Beatrice Harwood, "The National Estimates Approach to U.S. Fire Statistics," *Fire Technology*, May 1985, pp. 99–113.

Hanson, Eva Stottrup, "A Cohort Study on the Mortality of Firefighters," *British Journal of Industrial Medicine*, Vol. 47, 1990, pp. 805–809.

International Association of Fire Fighters, *Death and Injury Survey*, 1993–1998.

Jankovic, J., W. Jones, J. Burkhart, and G. Noonan, "Environmental Study of Firefighters," *Annals of Occupational Hygiene*, Vol. 35, No. 6, 1991, pp. 581–602.

Kales, S. N., G. N. Polyhrornopoulos, J. M. Aldrich, P. J. Mendoza, J. H. Suh, and D. C. Christiani, "Prospective Study of Hepatic, Renal, and Haematological Surveillance in Hazardous Materials Firefighters," *Occupational and Environmental Medicine*, Vol. 58, No. 2, February 2001, pp. 87–94.

Karter, Jr., Michael J., *Patterns of Firefighter Fireground Injuries*, Quincy, MA: National Fire Protection Association, February 2000.

Karter, Jr., Michael J., *U.S. Fire Department Profile Through 2000*, Quincy, MA: National Fire Protection Association, December 2001.

LaTourrette, T., D. J. Peterson, J. T. Bartis, B. A. Jackson, and A. Houser. *Protecting Emergency Responders, Volume 2: Community Views of Safety and Health Risks and Personal Protection Needs*, Santa Monica, Calif.: RAND Corporation, MR-1646-NIOSH, 2003.

Ma, Fangchao, David J. Lee, Lora E. Fleming, and Mustafa Dosemeci, "Race-Specific Cancer Mortality in U.S. Firefighters," *Journal of Occupational and Environmental Medicine*, Vol. 40, No. 12, December 1998, pp. 1134–1137.

Maguire, Brian J., Katherine L. Hunting, Gordon S. Smith, and Nadine R. Levick, "Occupational Fatalities in Emergency Medical Services: A Hidden Crisis," *Annals of Emergency Medicine*, Vol. 40, No. 6, December 2002, pp. 625–632.

Mayhew, Claire, "Occupational Health and Safety Risks Faced by Police Officers," *Trends and Issues in Crime and Criminal Justice*, No. 196, February 2001.

Mayhew, Claire, "Protecting the Occupational Health and Safety of Police Officers," *Trends and Issues in Crime and Criminal Justice*, No. 197, February 2001.

Murphy, Patrice L., Gary S. Sorock, Theodore K. Courtney, Barbara S. Webster, and Tom B. Leamon, "Injury and Illness in the American Workplace," *American Journal of Industrial Medicine*, Vol. 30, 1996, pp. 130–141.

National Center for Infectious Diseases, U.S. Department of Health and Human Services, *National Surveillance System for Health Care Workers*, database report. Obtained via personal communication from Adelisa Panlilio, March 12, 2002.

National EMS Memorial Service, *Notices of Line of Duty Death*, http://nemsms.org/notices.htm, accessed September 4, 2002.

National Fire Protection Association, *Fire Department Calls*, http://www.nfpa.org/pdf/os.fdcalls.pdf, accessed November 27, 2002.

National Fire Protection Association, *Firefighter Fatality Reports*, 1995–2000a.

National Fire Protection Association, *Firefighter Injury Reports*, 1995–2000b.

National Institute for Occupational Safety and Health, U.S. Department of Health and Human Services, Larry L. Jackson, unpublished data from the National Electronic Injury Surveillance System. Obtained via personal communication from Larry L. Jackson, 2001.

National Law Enforcement Officers Memorial Fund, database report. Obtained via personal communication from Berneta Spence, April 18, 2002a.

National Law Enforcement Officers Memorial Fund, *Year by Year Deaths*, http://nleomf.org/FactsFigures/yeardeaths.html, accessed August 20, 2002b.

National Public Safety Information Bureau, *National Directory of Fire Chiefs and EMS Administrators 2002*, Stevens Point, WI: Span Publishing, 2002a.

National Public Safety Information Bureau, *National Directory of Law Enforcement Administrators 2002*, Stevens Point, WI: Span Publishing, 2002b.

National Registry of Emergency Medical Technicians, *Practice Analysis*, 1999.

NFPA, *see* National Fire Protection Association

NIOSH, *see* National Institute for Occupational Safety and Health

NPSIB, *see* National Public Safety Information Bureau

Pepe, Paul E., James Jerger, Robert H. Miller, and Susan Jerger, "Accelerated Hearing Loss in Urban Emergency Medical Services Firefighters," *Annals of Emergency Medicine*, Vol. 14, May 1985, pp. 438–442.

Prezant, David J., Kerry J. Kelly, Kevin S. Malley, Manoj L. Karwa, Mary T. McLaughlin, Robin Hirschorn, and Audrey Brown, "Impact of a Modern Firefighting Protective Uniform on the Incidence and Severity of Burn Injuries in New York City Firefighters," *Journal of Occupational and Environmental Medicine*, Vol. 41, No. 6, June 1999, pp. 469–478.

Reaves, Brian A., *State and Local Police Departments, 1990*, NCJ-133284, Washington D.C.: U.S. Department of Justice, Office of Justice Programs, Bureau of Justice Statistics, 1992.

Reaves, Brian A., *Federal Law Enforcement Officers, 1993*, NCJ-151166, Washington D.C.: U.S. Department of Justice, Office of Justice Programs, Bureau of Justice Statistics, December 1994.

Reaves, Brian A., and Timothy C. Hart, *Federal Law Enforcement Officers 2000*, NCJ-187231, Washington, D.C.: U.S. Department of Justice, Office of Justice Programs, Bureau of Justice Statistics, July 2001.

Reaves, Brian A., and Matthew J. Hickman, *Census of State and Local Law Enforcement Agencies, 2000*, NCJ-194066, Washington D.C.: U.S. Department of Justice, Office of Justice Programs, Bureau of Justice Statistics, October 2002.

Reed, Elizabeth, Mohamud R. Daya, Jonathan Jui, Kathy Grellman, Leith Gerber, and Mark O. Loveless, "Occupational Infectious Disease Exposures in EMS Personnel," *Journal of Emergency Medicine*, Vol. 11, 1993, pp. 9–16.

Rosenstock, Linda, P. Demers, N. J. Heyer, S. Barnhart, "Respiratory Mortality Among Firefighters," *British Journal of Industrial Medicine*, Vol. 47, 1990, pp. 462–465.

Swanton, Bruce, "Research Brief: Police Work and Its Health Impacts," *Trends and Issues in Crime and Criminal Justice*, No. 7, October 1987.

U.S. Fire Administration, *National Fire Incident Reporting System 1998*, Firefighter Casualty Module.

U.S. Fire Administration, *Firefighter Fatalities in the United States in 1995*, Washington, D.C.: Federal Emergency Management Association, August 1996.

U.S. Fire Administration, *Firefighter Fatalities in the United States in 1996*, Washington, D.C.: Federal Emergency Management Association, August 1997.

U.S. Fire Administration, *Firefighter Fatalities in the United States in 1997*, Washington, D.C.: Federal Emergency Management Association, August 1998.

U.S. Fire Administration, *Firefighter Fatalities in the United States in 1998*, Washington, D.C.: Federal Emergency Management Association, August 1999.

U.S. Fire Administration, *Firefighter Fatalities in the United States in 1999*, Washington, D.C.: Federal Emergency Management Association, July 2000.

U.S. Fire Administration, *Firefighter Fatalities in the United States in 2000*, Washington, D.C.: Federal Emergency Management Association, August 2001.

U.S. Fire Administration, *USFA Releases Preliminary Firefighter Fatality Statistics for 2001*, http://www.usfa.fema.gov/dhtml/media/02-004.cfm, accessed December 13, 2002.

Appendix A: RAND Injury and Fatality Classification System

Because separate data sources typically have somewhat different methods of classifying injuries and fatalities by such factors as nature and cause of injury, RAND has integrated the various approaches in the data sources discussed in this analysis into a single classification system. Several charts detailing the crosswalk between RAND's classification system and the source systems, as well as any adjustments to the data, are included in this appendix.

Table A.1
Firefighter Nature of Injury Categories

RAND Analysis	IAFF Death and Injury Survey	NFPA Injury Reports	NFPA Fatality Reports	USFA Fatality Reports	NFIRS (note c)
Sprains, strains, other trauma	Sprains and strains	Strain, sprain, muscular pain	Internal trauma, gunshot, crushing	Internal trauma	16, 34, 40, 46, 51, 53
Fractures and dislocations	Fractures/ broken bones	Dislocation, fracture			21, 28, 29
Cuts and bruises	Lacerations and contusions	Wound, cut, bleeding, bruise	Amputations	Amputations	01, 02, 04, 13, 35, 44 (note d)
Eye injuries	Eye injuries	Eye Irritation			04 (note d)
Burns	Burns	Burns	Burns	Burns	05–08
Asphyxiation, hazmat inhalation, drowning, other respiratory	Exposure to hazardous materials – inhalation (note a)	Smoke or gas inhalation, other respiratory distress	Asphyxiation, drowning	Asphyxiation, including drowning	03, 20, 24, 47
Thermal Stress	Heat exhaustions/ heat strokes, cold injuries (note b)	Thermal stress	Heat stroke	Heat stroke	17, 22, 23, 30 (note e)
Cardiac	Cardiac abnormalities	Heart attack or stroke	Heart attack, stroke	Heart attack, stroke	10, 11, 52
Other	All other natures	All other natures	All other natures	All other natures	All other natures

Table A.2
Firefighter Cause of Injury Categories

RAND Analysis	NFPA Firefighter Injury Reports	NFPA Firefighter Fatality Reports	NFIRS (note c)
Struck by, contact with object	Stepped on, contact with, object, struck by object	Stepped on, contact with, object, struck by object	300–400, 403, 404, 406–409, 415–419, 499, 700–899
Fell, slipped, jumped	Fell, slipped, jumped	Fell	100–199, 600–699
Caught, trapped	Caught, trapped	Caught or trapped	200–299
Physical stress, overexertion	Overexertion, strain	Stress	500–599
Exposure to chemicals or radiation	Exposure to chemicals or radiation	Exposure	412–414
Exposure to fire products	Exposure to fire products		401, 402, 405, 410, 411
Exposure to extreme weather	Extreme weather		420
Other	All other causes	All other causes	All other causes

Table A.3
Firefighter Type of Duty Categories

RAND Analysis	IAFF Death and Injury Survey	NFPA Firefighter Injury Reports	NFPA Firefighter Fatality Reports	USFA Firefighter Fatality Reports
Fireground	Structural, non-structural fire suppression	Fireground	Fireground	Fireground operations
Responding, returning from alarm	Responding, returning from alarm	Responding or returning from an incident	Responding to, or returning from, alarms	Responding/returning
Nonfire emergency	EMS, technical rescue, HAZMAT	Nonfire emergency	Nonfire emergency	Nonfire emergency
Training	Training, physical fitness exercises	Training	Training	Training
Other	All other types of duty	All other types of duty	All other types of duty	All other types of duty

Table A.4
Firefighter Activity Categories

RAND Analysis	USFA Firefighter Fatality Reports	NFIRS (note c)
Fire attack	Advancing hose lines/fire attack, cutting fire breaks (wildland)	30–39
Search and rescue	Search and rescue	60–69
Ventilation and forcible entry	Ventilation, forcible entry	41–43
Salvage and overhaul	Salvage and overhaul	44, 45
Water supply (note f)	Water supply	72, 73
Incident scene support activities		70–79
Riding on or driving apparatus		10–29
Other	All other activities	All other activities

Table A.5
Police Cause-Event Categories

RAND Analysis	NLEOMF	BLS SOII (note g)
Assault, violence	AMBH, ARST, BEAT, NIFE, ROBB, SHOT, STRA	Assaults and violent acts by person(s)
Vehicle accident	AUTO, MOTO	Highway accident
Aircraft accident	AIRC, HELI	
Struck by vehicle	STRU	Pedestrian, nonpassenger struck by vehicle, mobile equipment
Fell, jumped	FALL	Falls
Physical stress, overexertion	PHYS	Bodily reaction and exertion
Exposure to fire and hazardous substances		Contact with temperature extremes; Exposure to caustic, noxious, or allergenic substances
Struck by, contact with object		Contact with objects and equipment
Other	All other causes	All other event/exposure categories

Notes

a) Other respiratory distress is not among the Death and Injury Survey categories. In the analysis, this number was scaled by the following factor: (count of smoke or gas inhalation + count of other respiratory distress for all types of duty in the NFPA firefighter injury reports)/(count of smoke or gas inhalation for all types of duty in the NFPA firefighter injury reports).

b) Based on comparison with the rates in NFPA injury reports and NFIRS, the heat stress reported in the Death and Injury Survey appears analogous to NFIRS codes 17 and 30. In the analysis, this number was scaled by the following factor: (all heat stress in Michael J. Karter, Jr., *Patterns of Firefighter Fireground Injuries*, NFPA, February 2000, adjusted by NFIRS 1998 as in note c)/(heat stress in codes 17 and 30).

c) Not all of these categories are included in Michael J. Karter, Jr., *Patterns of Firefighter Fireground Injuries*, NFPA, February 2000. For those RAND categories that include some but not all of the listed NFIRS codes for 1993–1997, the missing data are filled in from existing data in the same proportion as found in the NFIRS 1998 data.

d) Category 04 is divided by part of body. If part of body = 12, it is classified as "eye injuries," otherwise as "cuts and bruises."

e) Investigation of NFIRS 1998 data by cause and activity reveals that the majority of codes 22 and 23 can be considered heat stress; this amount can be estimated by 0.85 × (code 23 total value).

f) Water Supply is a subset of Incident Scene Support Activities.

g) Breakdowns for the BLS data were obtained at the 2-digit level of detail. Cause-event data for 99 percent of the injuries for 1998 through 2000 in New York State local government were publicly available at this level of detail. The 1 percent of injuries that were not reportable are included in the "other" category.

Appendix B: Fatality, Injury, Illness, and Exposure Numerical Data Tables

This appendix contains the numerical data that serve as the basis for the figures included in the text of the report.

Table B.1
Data Underlying Figure 4.1—Firefighter and Law
Enforcement Fatalities, 1980–2001

Year	Yearly Counts		September 11, 2001	
	Police	Fire	Police	Fire
1980	201	140		
1981	201	131		
1982	195	125		
1983	190	113		
1984	179	119		
1985	173	126		
1986	177	121		
1987	175	131		
1988	194	136		
1989	191	119		
1990	152	108		
1991	147	109		
1992	158	75		
1993	154	77		
1994	171	104		
1995	174	96		
1996	134	95		
1997	164	94		
1998	161	91		
1999	134	112		
2000	151	102		
2001	158	98	72	343
Average 1990–2001	154.8	96.8		

SOURCES: U.S. Fire Administration (2002), National Law
Enforcement Officers Memorial Fund (2002b).

Table B.2
Data Underlying Figure 4.2—Cause of Fatal Injuries for Firefighters,
Police, and EMS Workers (%)

Cause of Injury	Fire	Police	EMS
Assaults, violence	1	45	0
Vehicle accidents, struck by vehicle	18	40	30
Aircraft accident	4	4	57
Caught, trapped, exposure to fire products or chemicals	23	0	0
Physical stress, overexertion	46	7	7
Other	8	4	7
Total	100	100	100
Total sample size to calculate percentages	589[a]	1,575	46

SOURCE: NFPA (1995-2000a), National Law Enforcement Officers Memorial Fund (2002a), and National EMS Memorial Service (2002).

NOTES: Data are for 1995–2000 for firefighters, 1992–2001 for police, and 1998–2001 for EMS. Total percentages may not add due to rounding.

[a]Data averaged from two sources: 589 records from USFA, 579 records from NFPA. Near-complete overlap.

Table B.3
Data Underlying Figure 4.3—Nature of Injury for Firefighters, Police,
and EMS Injuries, 1996–1998

Nature of Injury	% of Fire Injuries	% of Police Injuries	% of EMS Injuries
Sprains, strains	36.2	36.6	48.3
Fractures, dislocations	3.8	4.7	—[a]
Lacerations	9.7	8.2	4.5
Punctures	2.4	3.7	9.9
Bruises, abrasions	16.2	28.3	17.6
Burns	6.7	1.1	—[a]
Asphyxiation, hazmat inhalation	7.1	1.7	—[a]
Other (1)	16.7	14.2	15.3
Other (2)	1.2	1.5	4.4
Total	100.0	100.0	100.0

SOURCE: L. L. Jackson, NIOSH, unpublished data. Total percentages may not add due to rounding.

NOTES: Other (1) is reported by the source, and corresponds to injuries coded as "other." Other (2) is not reported by the source, and corresponds to injuries coded by nature but occurring infrequently and therefore not coded above.

[a]Indicates these injuries are not broken out from the "other" category.

Table B.4
Data Underlying Figure 4.4—Type of Duty for Firefighter Injuries and Fatalities

	Injuries			
Type of Duty	NFPA Average Yearly Total	NFPA Percent	IAFF Percent	Combined Percent
Fireground	44,830	51	52	51
Responding to, returning from alarm	5,770	7	6	6
Non-fire emergency	13,700	16	17	16
Training	7,020	8	10	9
Other	16,610	19	16	17
Total	87,930	100	100	100

	Fatalities			
Type of Duty	NFPA Total	USFA Total	Combined Total	Combined Percent
Fireground	250	262	512	44
Responding to, returning from alarm	155	130	285	24
Non-fire emergency	61	72	133	11
Training	48	42	90	8
Other	65	83	148	13
Total	579	589	1,168	100

SOURCES: Fatalities from NFPA (1995–2000a) and U.S. Fire Administration (2002). Injuries from NFPA (1995–2000b) and IAFF (1993–1998).

NOTES: The values reported in the table are the average of the two sources. NFPA average yearly total is rounded to the nearest 10. Total percentages may not add due to rounding.

Table B.5
Data Underlying Figure 4.5—Firefighter Activity for Fireground Injuries and Fatalities

	Injuries				
	Patterns of Firefighter Fireground Injuries		Breakdown by severity level, calculated by applying NFIRS 1998 severity frequencies for each to *Patterns* totals for each activity		
			Minor	Moderate	Severe and Life-Threatening
Firefighter Activity	Total	Percent	% of Total	% of Total	% of Total
Fire attack	23,960	49	48	51	56
Search and rescue	1,710	4	3	4	3
Ventilation and forcible entry	4,760	10	10	10	11
Salvage and overhaul	7,600	16	17	13	8
Water supply	1,550	3	3	3	3
Other	9,040	19	19	19	19
Total	48,610	100	100	100	100

	Fatalities	
	USFA Firefighter Fatalities	
Firefighter Activity	Total	Percent
Fire attack	115	44
Search and rescue	34	13
Ventilation and forcible entry	13	5
Salvage and overhaul	4	2
Water supply	33	13
Other	63	24
Total	262	100

SOURCES: Fatalities from U.S. Fire Administration (1996–2001). Injuries from Karter (2000) adjusted by analysis of the NFIRS 1998 firefighter casualty module, rounded to the nearest 10.

NOTES: Totals may not add due to rounding. The NFIRS 1998 data were used to estimate the incidence of activities unreported in Karter (2000) and to reclassify certain natures based on additional information contained in the NFIRS database. Injuries were sorted into minor, moderate, and severe using percentages calculated from the NFIRS 1998 firefighter casualty module for fireground injuries. Severe injuries are based on a sample of less than 200 injuries, and therefore there is significant uncertainty involved in calculating both the breakdown of severe injuries by activity and the percentage of injuries occurring during each activity that are severe. Investigation of the NFIRS 1998 data indicates that many of the injuries in the "other" category occurred while picking up or carrying tools on the fireground, or have activity unreported or classified as "other." Total percentages may not add due to rounding.

Table B.6
Data Underlying Figure 4.6—Firefighter Fireground Injuries by Cause

Cause of Injury	NFPA Firefighter Injury Reports (per year average)		Patterns of Firefighter Fireground Injuries		Combined Percent	Percent of each severity level, calculated by applying NFIRS 1998 severity frequencies for each to Patterns totals for each activity		
	Total	Percent	Total	Percent		Minor	Moderate	Severe
Struck by, contact with object	8,600	19	12,110	25	22	25	18	10
Vehicle related[a]			230	0.5	0.5	0.4	0.4	2
Fell, jumped	10,820	24	9,790	20	22	23	24	7
Caught, trapped	600	1	2,210	5	3	3	3	3
Exposure to fire products, chemicals, extreme weather	9,570	21	11,150	23	22	21	24	35
Physical stress, overexertion	12,300	27	11,080	23	25	24	28	37
Other	2,940	7	2,270	5	6	4	3	8
Total	44,830	100	48,610	100	100	100	100	100

SOURCE: NFPA (1995-2000b) and Karter (2000) adjusted by NFIRS 1998 data.

NOTES: The NFIRS 1998 data were used to estimate the incidence of activities unreported in Karter (2000) and to reclassify certain natures based on additional information contained in the NFIRS database. The values reported are the average of the two sources. Injuries were sorted into minor, moderate, and severe using percentages calculated from the NFIRS 1998 firefighter casualty module for fireground injuries. Severe injuries are based on a sample of less than 200 injuries, and therefore there is significant uncertainty involved in calculating both the breakdown of severe injuries by activity and the percentage of injuries occurring during each activity that are severe. Total percentages may not add due to rounding. Counts should be considered approximate, and are rounded to the nearest 10.

[a]"Vehicle related" is a subcategory of "Struck by, contact with object."

Table B.7
Data Underlying Figure 4.7—Breakdown of Firefighter Occupational Injury Retirements (%)

Retirement Cause		1993	1994	1995	1996	1997	1998	% of Total[a]
Noninjury Retirements		**67.6**	**79.7**	**75.9**	**69.8**	**64.5**	**78.4**	**73.0**
Injury Retirements		**25.4**	**14.4**	**15.7**	**17.1**	**23.7**	**15.7**	**18.5**
Percentage of injury retirements	Back injury	44.2	52.6	56.3	52.9	44.7	54.5	9.3
	Limb/Torso injury	36.5	28.7	29.2	_b	_b	_b	5.8
	Leg/Hips/ Abdomen injury				19.3	19.1	18.9	—
	Arm/Shoulder/ Chest injury				8.5	11.8	12.5	—
	Foot injury	4.2	0.9	2.3	2.1	2.6	3.0	0.5
	Hand injury	6.1	1.1	2.6	2.7	2.9	0.8	0.6
	Head/Face injury	6.8	1.1	6.4	2.4	0.7	1.9	0.7
	Location unknown	2.2	15.6	3.2	12.1	18.2	8.3	1.8
Illness Retirements		**7.0**	**5.9**	**8.4**	**13.1**	**11.8**	**5.9**	**8.5**
Percentage of illness retirements	Heart disease	44.7	50.3	47.0	47.0	55.8	55.0	4.2
	Lung disease	10.0	9.0	20.8	23.3	20.4	19.0	1.5
	Cancer	9.3	14.5	14.2	17.0	10.6	12.0	1.1
	Hearing loss	9.3	5.5	8.7	3.2	4.4	2.0	0.5
	Mental stress	9.3	12.4	6.0	4.7	6.2	10.0	0.5
	Other disease	17.3	8.3	3.3	4.0	2.7	2.0	0.5

SOURCE: International Association of Fire Fighters, IAFF Death and Injury Survey (1993-1998)

NOTE: Total percentages may not add due to rounding [a]Percent of all retirements, weighted by estimated number of total retirements in each year (see table below for population adjustments). [b]After 1996, Limb/Torso injuries were broken down into Leg/Hip/Abdomen and Arm/Shoulder/Chest.

Population Adjustments	1993	1994	1995	1996	1997	1998
IAFF population sampled	93,786	96,431	89,595	107,988	105,568	97,335
Injury and illness retirements in IAFF sample	695	497	526	584	682	364
Injury and illness retirements as a percentage of all retirements	32.4%	20.3%	24.1%	30.2%	35.5%	21.6%
Career firefighter population (from NFPA)	259,650	265,700	260,850	266,300	275,700	278,300
Estimated total retirements in firefighter population	5,940	6,750	6,350	4,770	5,020	4,820

Table B.8
Data Underlying Figure 4.8—Firefighter Fireground Injuries by Nature, Severity, Cause and Activity

The data that serve as the basis for Figure 4.8 are drawn from the National Fire Incident Reporting System (NFIRS) database for 1998. The data tables included here summarize the analysis of the data drawn from that database and creation of the matrix showing the cause and activity for moderate and severe fireground injuries included in the text.

There are 7,072 records in the NFIRS 1998 firefighter casualty module. Of these, 6,651 were used in the analysis because the other records contained no information on the cause of injury, nature of injury, or firefighter activity. Of those records, 5,389 occurred on the fireground, with the rest occurring off the fireground or with location classified as "other" or "unknown."

On the following tables, NFIRS code numbers for nature of injury, severity of injury, and firefighter activity used in the 1998 database are included. Keys to those code numbers are included after the data tables. Note that, changes have occurred in the codes used in NFIRS since 1998. As a result, the codes included here do not completely correspond with the codes in use now.

Table B.8a
Firefighter Injuries by Cause and Severity (All Injuries)

| Cause | Severity | | | | | | | | Total |
	0	1	2	3	4	5	6	(blank)	
Other/unknown	11	762	304	20	3	1	3	6	1,110
Fell		664	393	11					1,068
Caught, trapped		170	108	6			3		287
Struck by object (nonvehicle)		520	289	3	1	1	2		816
Struck by vehicle		8	7	3					18
Contact with object (non-exposure)		457	236	10			1		704
Exposure to fire products		605	314	47	1	1	1		969
Exposure to chemicals or radiation	17	59	94	3					173
Contagious disease		3	3		2				8
Extreme weather		9	14	2					25
Physical stress or overexertion		748	536	52	5	1			1,342
Jumped		47	22						69
Vehicle accident		17	17	1					35
Assault		19	8						27
Total	28	4,088	2,345	158	12	4	10	6	6,651

Table B.8b
Firefighter Injuries by Cause and Severity (Fireground Injuries)

| | Severity | | | | | | | |
Cause	0	1	2	3	4	5	6	Total
Other/unknown	6	253	111	16	2	1	3	392
Fell		626	364	10				1,000
Caught, trapped		155	82	6			3	246
Struck by object (nonvehicle)		497	230	3	1	1	2	734
Struck by vehicle		7	4	3				14
Contact with object (nonexposure)		430	128	10				568
Exposure to fire products		587	307	45	1	1	1	942
Exposure to chemicals or radiation	16	57	88	1				162
Contagious disease		3	2		2			7
Extreme weather		9	14	2				25
Physical stress or overexertion		705	438	47	5	1		1,196
Jumped		46	20					66
Vehicle accident		7	3					10
Assault		19	8					27
Total	**22**	**3,401**	**1,799**	**143**	**11**	**4**	**9**	**5,389**

Table B.8c
Firefighter Injuries by Nature and Severity (All Injuries)

| Nature | Nature Code | Severity | | | | | | | (blank) | Total |
		0	1	2	3	4	5	6		
Asphyxiation, hazmat inhalation	03	12	122	131	23			1	2		291
Burns	Total		546	328	13				1		888
	05		15	17							32
	06		4	5	2						11
	07		440	282	11				1		734
	08		87	24							111
Other respiratory	Total		63	54	10						127
	20		63	54	9						126
	47				1						1
Cardiac	Total		13	45	28	5	2	3			96
	10		1			3	2	3			9
	11		12	45	27	2					86
	52				1						1
Other trauma, non-fracture	Total		55	35	4	1	1	2			98
	16		20	14		1	1				36
	31		24	8	1						33

Table B.8c—continued

Nature	Nature Code	Severity								Total
		0	1	2	3	4	5	6	(blank)	
	34		10	9	3					22
	46		1	4				2		7
Likely thermal stress	Total		210	143	31	1				385
	17		74	58	21	1				154
	22		10	6						16
	23		122	79	10					211
	30		4							4
Fractures and dislocations	Total		36	103	8	1				148
	21		19	27	2					48
	28		16	75	6	1				98
	29		1	1						2
Sprains, strains, non-fracture trauma	Total		1291	786	15					2,092
	40		468	265	6					739
	51		763	486	8					1,257
	53		60	35	1					96
Cuts and bruises	Total		819	314	5					1,138
	01		125	20	1					146
	02		6	2	1					9
	04		10	1						11
	13		223	78						301
	35		326	185	3					514
	44		129	28						157
Eye injury	Total		95	23						118
	04		16	10						26
	27		79	13						92
Other, unknown	Total	16	838	383	21	4		2	6	1,270
	??		14	6	1	1				22
	00		495	95	5			1	6	602
	12		2							2
	14					1				1
	26		1							1
	32		10	4	1					15
	33		1	1						2
	36		1							1
	37		17	9						26
	38			1						1
	41			2						2
	42		13	6	1					20
	45			3	1					4
	48		1							1
	49		16	16	2					34
	50		13	6	1					20
	54		1	3	2					6
	55		5	10						15
	59			1						1
	98	11	97	47		2				157
	99	5	133	169	7			1		315
	blank		18	4						22
Total		28	4,088	2,345	158	12	4	10	6	6,651

Table B.8d
Firefighter Injuries by Nature and Severity (Fireground Only)

Nature	Nature Code	Severity							Total
		0	1	2	3	4	5	6	
Asphyxiation	03	8	115	97	21		1	2	244
Burns	Total		534	241	12			1	788
	05		15	17					32
	06		4	5	2				11
	07		430	195	10			1	636
	08		85	24					109
Other respiratory	Total		60	52	8				120
	20		60	52	7				119
	47				1				1
Cardiac	Total		10	37	26	5	2	3	83
	10		1			3	2	3	9
	11		9	37	25	2			73
	52				1				1
Other trauma, non-fracture	Total		46	32	3	1	1	2	85
	16		17	13		1	1		32
	31		19	7	1				27
	34		9	9	2				20
	46		1	3				2	6
Likely thermal stress	Total		201	134	31	1			367
	17		73	56	21	1			151
	22		8	5					13
	23		116	73	10				199
	30		4						4
Fractures and dislocations	Total		33	85	7				125
	21		16	25	1				42
	28		16	59	6				81
	29		1	1					2
Sprains, strains, non-fracture trauma	Total		1,191	645	11				1,847
	40		430	247	4				681
	51		705	366	7				1,078
	53		56	32					88
Cuts and bruises	Total		768	238	4				1,010
	01		107	18	1				126
	02		5	2	1				8
	04		10	1					11
	13		209	70					279
	35		312	119	2				433
	44		125	28					153
Eye injuries	Total		87	23					110
	04		14	10					24
	27		73	13					86
Other/ unknown	Total	14	356	215	20	4		1	610
	??		7	6	1	1			15
	00		64	59	5			1	129
	12		1						1
	14					1			1
	26		1						1

Table B.8d—continued

Nature	Nature Code	Severity							Total
		0	**1**	**2**	**3**	**4**	**5**	**6**	
Other/	32		8	2	1				11
unknown	33		1	1					2
	36		1						1
	37		17	6					23
	41			2					2
	42		12	4	1				17
	45			3	1				4
	49		13	15	2				30
	50		9	4	1				14
	54		1	3	2				6
	55		5	10					15
	59		1						1
	98	9	81	44		2			136
	99	5	122	52	6				185
	blank		13	3					16
Total		**22**	**3,401**	**1,799**	**143**	**11**	**4**	**9**	**5,389**

Table B.8e
Analysis of Avulsion Injuries—Assignment of Avulsions to RAND Injury Categories and Types of Duty

RAND Nature of Injury Category	NFIRS Body Part	Type of Duty	Severity		Total
			1	**2**	
		Fireground	14	10	24
Eye Injuries	Eyes	Enroute/returning	1		1
		(blank)	1		1
		Total	**16**	**10**	**26**
Cut/Bruise	All other body parts	Fireground	10	1	
		Total	**10**	**1**	**11**
		Fireground	24	11	35
Total	All body parts	Enroute/returning	1		1
		(blank)	1		1
		Total	**26**	**11**	**37**

Table B.8f
Assignment of Dizziness, Fainting and Disorientation to RAND Injury
Categories by NFIRS Cause (Fireground Injuries Only)

RAND Nature of Injury Category	NFIRS Nature	NFIRS Cause	Severity				Total
			1	2	3	4	
Thermal stress	Disorientation	Extreme weather		1			1
		Exposure to heat		2			2
		Physical stress, Overexertion	3	2			5
		Total	**3**	**5**			**8**
	Dizziness/ Fainting	Extreme weather	4	1			5
		Exposure to heat	12	14	1		27
		Physical stress, Overexertion	70	40	3		113
		Total	**86**	**55**	**4**		**145**
Other natures	Disorientation	Caught/trapped	2				2
		Fell	1				1
		Contact with object	1				1
		Struck by object	1				1
		Total	**5**				**5**
	Dizziness/ fainting	Exposure to smoke	10	5	4		19
		Exposure to chemicals	1	1	1		3
		Vehicle accident	1				1
		Caught/trapped	1				1
		Fell	1	1			2
		Struck by object	3	1			4
		Total	**17**	**8**	**5**		**30**

For injuries where no NFIRS cause was specified, counts were allocated to thermal stress (81%) and other natures (19%) based on the corresponding fraction of injuries with known cause:

Disorientation				1			1
Dizziness/ Fainting			13	10	1		24
Total			**13**	**11**	**1**		**25**

Table B.8g
Firefighter Injuries by Activity and Severity (All Injuries)

Firefighter Activity	Activity Code	Severity								Total
		0	1	2	3	4	5	6	(blank)	
Salvage and overhaul	Total	2	452	189	8	1				652
	44		41	19	1					61
	45	2	411	170	7	1				591
Ventilation and forcible entry	Total		273	146	12	1				432
	41		79	49	2					130
	42		52	43	5					100
	43		142	54	5	1				202
Vehicle	Total		198	145	16	2		1		362
	10		4	15				1		20
	11		12	6	1					19
	12		3	1						4
	13		16	23	1					40
	14		4							4
	15		3							3
	16		2	3	1	1				7
	17		62	28	3					93
	19		4	1						5
	20		5	2						7
	21		16	16	2	1				35
	22		5							5
	23		1	5	1					7
	25		41	36	6					83
	26		5	5						10
	27		5		1					6
	29		10	4						14
Fire attack	Total	16	1,690	1,233	82	5	2	6		3,034
	30	4	216	415	6			1		642
	31		1,129	619	64	4	2	5		1,823
	32		28	14						42
	33		12	6	1					19
	34		196	119	7	1				323
	39	12	109	60	4					185
Search and rescue	Total		111	89	5	1				206
	60		4	17						21
	61		71	44	5					120
	62		32	26		1				59
	69		4	2						6
Incident scene support activities	Total		391	186	9			2		588
	51		13	5						18
	52		13	6						19
	53		1	1						2
	70		32	16	1					49
	71		3	1				1		5
	72		35	11						46
	73		69	35	4					108
	74		77	47	2					126
	75		77	27						104
	76		5	4						9

Table B.8g—continued

Firefighter Activity	Activity Code	Severity							(blank)	Total
		0	1	2	3	4	5	6		
Incident scene	77		3	1						4
support activities	79		63	32	2				1	98
Other, unknown	**Total**	**10**	**973**	**357**	**26**	**2**	**2**	**1**	**6**	**1,377**
	??		11	2						13
	00	8	477	63	5				6	559
	35		1							1
	36		3							3
	37		5	5	1					11
	40	2	144	106	5					257
	49		122	51	4			1		178
	50		18	9						27
	54		20	21	1					42
	55		1	2						3
	56		5	6			1			12
	59		22	22						44
	63		4							4
	65		5	7						12
	67		1							1
	68		1							1
	80		1	4						5
	81		14	5						19
	82		2	2						4
	83			1						1
	84		3	2						5
	85		2	3	2					7
	88			1						1
	89		7	3	1					11
	91		33	12	3					48
	92		6	3			1			10
	93		2							2
	94		5	3	1					9
	95		5							5
	99		42	20	2	2				66
	(blank)		11	4	1					16
Total		**28**	**4,088**	**2,345**	**158**	**12**	**4**	**10**	**6**	**6,651**

Table B.8h
Firefighter Injuries by Activity and Severity (Fireground Only)

Firefighter Activity	Activity Code	Severity							Total
		0	1	2	3	4	5	6	
Salvage and overhaul	Total	2	442	179	8	1			632
	44		40	17	1				58
	45	2	402	162	7	1			574
Ventilation and forcible entry	Total		265	144	12	1			422
	41		78	48	2				128
	42		47	43	5				95
	43		140	53	5	1			199
Vehicle	Total		147	90	11	1			249
	10		1	1					2
	11		1	2					3
	12		1						1
	13		2	7					9
	14		3						3
	15		2						2
	16		1						1
	17		59	20	3				82
	19		2	1					3
	20		4	2					6
	21		9	10	1	1			21
	22		2						2
	23		1	3					4
	25		40	35	6				81
	26		5	5					10
	27		5		1				6
	29		9	4					13
Fire attack	Total	16	1,624	906	78	5	2	6	2637
	30	4	196	102	6			1	309
	31		1,095	610	62	4	2	5	1778
	32		27	13					40
	33		12	6	1				19
	34		189	115	7	1			312
	39	12	105	60	2				179
Search and rescue	Total		108	72	4	1			185
	60		4	2					6
	61		68	42	4				114
	62		32	26		1			59
	69		4	2					6
Incident scene support activities	Total		373	178	9			2	562
	51		13	4					17
	52		12	6					18
	53		1	1					2
	70		27	14	1				42
	71		3	1				1	5
	72		34	11					45
	73		68	34	4				106
	74		75	47	2				124
	75		71	26					97
	76		5	4					9

TableB.8h—continued

Firefighter Activity	Activity Code	Severity							Total
		0	1	2	3	4	5	6	
Incident scene	77		3	1					4
support activities	79		61	29	2			1	93
Other, unknown	**Total**	**4**	**442**	**230**	**21**	**2**	**2**	**1**	**702**
	??		8	2					10
	00	2	21	13	3				39
	36		3						3
	37		5	5	1				11
	40	2	130	72	5				209
	49		117	45	4			1	167
	50		18	9					27
	54		20	21	1				42
	55		1	2					3
	56		5	6			1		12
	59		22	22					44
	63		4						4
	65		5	4					9
	67		1						1
	68		1						1
	82		1						1
	89			1	1				2
	91		33	12	3				48
	92		5	3			1		9
	93		1						1
	94		5	2	1				8
	95		2						2
	99		32	9	2	2			45
	(blank)		2	2					4
Total		**22**	**3,401**	**1,799**	**143**	**11**	**4**	**9**	**5,389**

Table B.8i

Codes Identifying Primary Apparent Symptom of Injury in the NFIRS 1998 Database

01 Abrasion
02 Amputation
03 Asphyxiation (included is smoke inhalation)
04 Avulsion (included is avulsion of eye, eye trauma, out of socket)
05 Burn: chemical
06 Burn: electrical
07 Burn: thermal
08 Burn: scald
09 Cancer
10 Cardiac arrest
11 Cardiac symptoms
12 Chills
13 Contusion/bruise – minor trauma
14 Convulsion/seizure: unspecified (included is petite mal)
15 Convulsion/seizure: systemic (included is grand mal)
16 Crushing
17 Dehydration
18 Diabetic coma
19 Diabetic shock
20 Difficulty breathing/shortness of breath
21 Dislocation
22 Disorientation
23 Dizziness/fainting/weakness
24 Drowning
25 Drug overdose
26 Fever
27 Foreign body, obstruction
28 Fracture: closed
29 Fracture: open
30 Frostbite
31 Hemorrhaging, bleeding
32 Hypersensitivity (included is allergic reaction to medicines)
33 Impairment similar to that caused by alcohol
34 Internal trauma (closed blunt)
35 Laceration, cut
36 Mental disorder
37 Nausea
38 Obstetrics – delivery
39 Obstetrics – miscarriage
40 Pain only
41 Paralysis
42 Parasthesia, numbness, tingling
43 Pneumonia
44 Pucture/wound: penetrating (included are stab wounds)
45 Poison not listed elsewhere
46 Projectile wound – high velocity (included are gunshot wounds)
47 Respiratory arrest
48 Shock: anaphylactic
49 Shock: electrical
50 Sickness

Table B.8i—continued

51 Sprain, strain
52 Stroke (C.V.A.)
53 Swelling
54 Unconscious
55 Vomiting
59 Other long-term illness
98 No apparent symptom
99 Apparent symptom not classified above
00 Apparent symptom undetermined or not reported

Table B.8j
Codes Identifying Firefighter Activity in the NFIRS 1998 Database

1   Riding Vehicle

11	Boarding fire apparatus, emergency vehicle
12	Riding fire apparatus: standing
13	Riding fire apparatus: sitting
14	Riding fire apparatus: position unknown
15	Riding other emergency vehicle (included are ambulances, boats, planes, etc.)
16	Riding nonemergency vehicle
17	Getting off fire apparatus, emergency vehicle
18	Jumping from aircraft
19	Riding vehicle not classified above
10	Riding vehicle; insufficient information classify further

2   Driving/Operating Apparatus

21	Driving fire apparatus
22	Tillering ladder truck
23	Driving other emergency vehicle (included are ambulances, boats)
24	Flying aircraft
25	Operating engine/pump
26	Operating ladder truck, elevated platform
27	Operating other apparatus/equipment (included are power winches, stationary generators, etc.)
29	Driving/operating not classified above
20	Driving/operating; insufficient information classify further

3   Extinguishing Fire/Neutralizing Incident

31	Handling charged hose lines
32	Using hand extinguishers
33	Operating master stream device
34	Using hand tools in extinguishment activity
35	Removing power lines
36	Removing flammable liquids/chemicals
37	Shutting off utilities, gas lines, etc.
39	Extinguishing fire/neutralizing incident not classified
30	Extinguishing fire/neutralizing incident; insufficient information classify further

4   Suppression Support

41	Forcible entry
42	Ventilation with power tools
43	Ventilation with hand tools
44	Salvage
45	Overhaul
49	Suppression support not classified
40	Suppression support; insufficient information classify further

5   Access/Egress

51	Carrying ground ladder
52	Raising ground ladder
53	Lowering ground ladder
54	Climbing ladder
55	Scaling
56	Escaping fire/hazard
59	Access/egress not classified
50	Access/egress; insufficient information classify further

6   Rescue

61	Searching for fire victim
62	Rescue of fire victim
63	Rescue of non-fire victim
64	Water rescue
65	Providing emergency medical care
66	Diving operations
67	Extraction with power tools
68	Extraction with hand tools
69	Rescue not classified above
60	Rescue; insufficient information classify further

7   Miscellaneous Incident Scene Activity

71	Directing traffic
72	Catching hydrant
73	Laying hose
74	Moving tools or equipment around scene
75	Picking up tools, equipment, hose on scene
76	Setting up lighting
77	Operating portable pump
79	Miscellaneous incident scene activity not classified above
70	Miscellaneous incident scene activity; insufficient information classify further

8   Station Activity

81	Moving about station, alarm sounding
82	Moving about station, normal activity
83	Station maintenance
84	Vehicle maintenance
85	Equipment maintenance
86	Physical fitness activity: supervised
87	Physical fitness activity: unsupervised
88	Training activity or drill
89	Station activity not classified above
80	Station activity; insufficient information classify further

9   Other Activity

91	Incident investigation: during incident
92	Incident investigation: after incident
93	Inspection activity
94	Administrative work
95	Communication work
99	Activity at time injury/accident not classified above
00	Activity at time injury/accident undetermined or unreported

Table B.8k
Severity of Injury Codes in the NFIRS 1998 Database

1. Minor	The patient is not in danger of death or permanent disability. Immediate medical care is not necessary.
2. Moderate	There is little danger of death or permanent disability. Quick medical care is advisable. This category includes injuries such as fractures or lacerations requiring sutures.
3. Severe	The situation is potentially life threatening if the condition remains uncontrolled. Immediate medical care is necessary even though body processes may still be functioning and vital signs may be normal.
4. Life Threat	Death is imminent: body processes and vital signs are not normal. Immediate medical care is necessary. This category includes such as severe hemorrhaging, severe multiple trauma, and multiple internal injuries.
5 & 6. Fatality	Death occurs either on arrival at the scene or subsequently.

Table B.8l
Extracted Data for Figure 4.8—Injury Incidence Matrix for Moderate and Severe Firefighter Fireground Injuries by Cause and Activity

Activity	Nature of Injury	Total Moderate and Severe Injuries by Cause of Injury					
		Caught, Trapped	Fell, Jumped	Exposure to Fire Products	Physical Stress	Struck by, Contact with Object	Exposure to Chemicals
Salvage and overhaul	Asphyxiation	1				1	3
	Other		2	2	6	8	
	Burns	1		1		2	3
	Other respiratory			1	1	1	
	Cardiac				5		
	Other trauma, nonfracture	1	2			1	
	Thermal stress				8		
	Fractures and dislocations		5		1	1	
	Sprains and strains	3	23		30	17	1
	Cuts and bruises	1	4	1	1	26	
	Eye injury					9	
Ventilation and forcible entry	Asphyxiation			10	2		
	Other			2	4	4	2
	Burns			1	1	1	
	Other respiratory			1	1		
	Cardiac				4		
	Other trauma, non-fracture	1				2	
	Thermal stress			7	6		
	Fractures and dislocations	1	1		2	3	
	Sprains and strains		17		22	9	
	Cuts and bruises	1	1	1	4	29	
	Eye Injury					1	
Search and rescue	Asphyxiation			8		1	
	Other			2		1	
	Burns			15			
	Other respiratory			1	1		
	Cardiac				1		
	Other trauma, non-fracture		1				
	Thermal stress			4	1		
	Fractures and dislocations		4			1	
	Sprains and strains	1	3	2	12	3	
	Cuts and bruises		4		1	5	

Table B.8l—continued

Activity	Nature of Injury	Caught, Trapped	Fell, Jumped	Exposure to Fire Products	Physical Stress	Struck by, Contact with Object	Exposure to Chemicals
				Total Moderate and Severe Injuries by Cause of Injury			
Incident scene support activities	Asphyxiation			4			5
	Other		3		3	12	
	Burns	1	1	3	1	1	1
	Other respiratory				2		
	Cardiac				5		
	Other trauma, non-fracture	3				2	
	Thermal stress			1	7		1
	Fractures and dislocations		7			2	
	Sprains and strains	1	32		37	6	
	Cuts and bruises	2	8			16	
	Eye injury				1		
Fire Attack	Asphyxiation	3		44	2	1	14
	Other	2	13	28	25	21	34
	Burns	28	5	126	1	24	2
	Other respiratory			9	15	6	3
	Cardiac			5	??	1	
	Other trauma, nonfracture	4	4		2	5	
	Thermal stress		1	32	56		1
	Fractures and dislocations	5	18		7	9	
	Sprains and strains	12	94	2	123	39	
	Cuts and bruises	3	18	1	4	50	
	Eye injury					9	
Vehicle	Asphyxiation			3		1	1
	Other		1	1	4	2	
	Burns		1	1		2	
	Other respiratory			1		1	
	Cardiac			1	1		
	Other trauma, nonfracture	1				1	
	Thermal stress			2	2		
	Fractures and dislocations		8		1		
	Sprains and strains		33		7	4	
	Cuts and bruises	2	1			9	
	Eye injury			1			

Table B.9
Data Underlying Figures 4.9 and 4.10—Cause of Injury for Police Lost Work Time Injuries and Fatalities and Severity of Police Lost Work Time Injuries by Cause of Injury

	Fatalities		Injuries, Local Government, Police and Detectives, New York State, 1998–2000		
Cause	Total	Percent	Average Annual	Percent	Severity
Assault, violence	709	45	2,273	27	4
Vehicle accident	493	31	1,348	16	4
Aircraft accident	62	4	—a		
Struck by vehicle	143	9	19	0.2	5
Fell, jumped	27	2	1,587	19	5
Physical stress, overexertion	103	7	2,080	25	5
Exposure to fire and hazardous substances	—a		99	1	4
Struck by, contact with object	—a		810	10	3
Other	38	2	213	3	
Total	1,575	100	8,429	100	4

SOURCES: Fatalities from National Law Enforcement Officers Memorial Fund (2002a). Injuries from Survey of Occupational Injuries and Illnesses, Bureau of Labor Statistics (2003b).

NOTES: Data include police and detectives (occupation code 418), State of New York, at the local government level, for the years 1998–2000. "Struck by vehicle" refers to officers struck while not inside a vehicle. Severity is based on the median days away from work produced by each injury type. The overall severity measure reported here is the median of the three median measurements for the three years examined. Total percentages may not add due to rounding.

[a]Indicates these injuries and fatalities are not broken out from the "other" category.

Table B.10

Data Underlying Figure 4.11—Injury Incidence and Severity of Police Lost Work Time Injuries by Cause

RAND Cause Category	BLS Event or Exposure (Code and Category Name)	1998			1999			2000			1998–2000			
		Count	Percent of Total	Median of Days Away	Count	Percent of Total	Median of Days Away	Count	Percent of Total	Median of Days Away	Count	Annual Average	Percent of Total	Median of Days Away
Struck by, contact with object	0 Contact with objects and equipment	804	10	3	712	8	3	914	11	4	2,430	810	10	3
Fell, jumped	1 Falls	1,262	16	6	1,883	21	5	1,617	19	5	4,762	1,587	19	5
Physical stress, overexertion	2 Bodily reaction and exertion	3,265	41	4	1,618	18	5	1,352	16	6	6,240	2,080	25	5
Exposure to fire and hazardous substances	32 Contact with temperature extremes	67	1	6										
	34 Exposure to caustic, noxious, or allergenic substances	50	1	3	75	1	4	105	1	2				
	Total	**117**	**1**	**5**	**75**	**1**	**4**	**105**	**1**	**2**	**297**	**99**	**1**	**4**
Vehicle accident (including struck by vehicle)	41 Highway accident	1,652	21	4	1,161	13	4	1,231	15	5	4,044	1,348	16	4
	43 Pedestrian, nonpassenger struck by vehicle, mobile equipment				27	0.3	4	30	0.4	6	57	19	0.2	5
	Total	**1,652**	**21**	**4**	**1,188**	**13**	**4**	**1,251**	**15**	**5**	**4,091**	**1,364**	**16**	**4**
Assault, violence	61 Assaults and violent acts by person(s)	616	8	4	3,272	36	3	2,932	35	4	6,820	2,273	27	4
Other	All other event/exposures	240	3	—	242	3	—	166	2	—	648	216	3	4
	Total	**7,960**	**100**	**4**	**8,990**	**100**	**4**	**8,338**	**100**	**4**	**25,288**	**8,429**	**100**	**4**

SOURCE: Survey of Occupational Injuries and Illnesses, Bureau of Labor Statistics (2003b), data for police and detectives, State of New York, at the local government level, for the years 1998–2000.

NOTE: Total percentages may not add due to rounding.

Table B.11
Data Underlying Figure 4.11—Injury Incidence by Cause and Nature of Police Lost-Work-Time Injuries

RAND Cause Category	BLS Event or Exposure (Code and Category Name)	RAND Nature	BLS Nature Codes (Specified Below)	1998 Count	1999 Count	2000 Count	1998–2000 Count
Struck by, contact with object	0 Contact with objects and equipment	Trauma	00, 01, 02, 06, 08, 09	308	131	425	864
		Cuts/bruises	03, 04	373	581	485	1,438
		Symptoms of illness	41	64			64
		Total		**804**	**712**	**914**	**2,430**
Fell, jumped	1 Falls	Trauma	00, 01, 02, 06, 08, 09	925	1,542	1,363	3,830
		Cuts/bruises	03, 04	274	310	239	823
		Symptoms of illness	41	61		10	71
		Total		**1,262**	**1,883**	**1,617**	**4,762**
Physical stress, overexertion	2 Bodily reaction and exertion	Trauma	00, 01, 02, 06, 08, 09	2,554	1,567	1,342	5,464
		Cuts/bruises	03, 04		37		37
		Symptoms of illness	41	705			705
		Total		**3,269**	**1,618**	**1,352**	**6,239**
Exposure to fire and hazardous substances	32 Contact with temperature extremes	Burns	05	113			113
	34 Exposure to caustic, noxious, or allergenic substances	Symptoms of illness	41		35	32	67
		Trauma	00, 01, 02, 06, 08, 09		32		32
		Total		**117**	**75**	**105**	**297**
Vehicle accident	41 Highway accident	Trauma	00, 01, 02, 06, 08, 09	1,255	961	1,189	3,405
		Cuts/bruises	03, 04	397	200	19	615
		Total		**1,652**	**1,161**	**1,231**	**4,044**
Assault, violence	61 Assaults and violent acts by person(s)	Trauma	00, 01, 02, 06, 08, 09	327	2,666	2,230	5,223
		Cuts/bruises	03, 04	279	603	642	1,524
		Symptoms of illness	41			53	53
		Total		**616**	**3,272**	**2,932**	**6,820**

SOURCE: Survey of Occupational Injuries and Illnesses, Bureau of Labor Statistics (2003b).

NOTE: Data are for police and detectives, State of New York, at the local government level, for the years 1998–2000. Total percentages may not add due to rounding. Totals are higher than the sums of intermediate counts because other natures and nature unknown are omitted from the table. Struck by vehicle was not included with vehicle accidents because the count of this event/exposure was too small to analyze. Blank cell does not necessarily mean zero, but "too few cases to report."

BLS Name Codes

Code	Description
00	Traumatic injuries and disorders, unspecified
01	Traumatic injuries to bones, nerves, spinal cord
02	Traumatic injuries to muscles, tendons, ligaments, joints, etc
03	Open wounds
04	Surface wounds and bruises
05	Burns
06	Intracranial injuries
08	Multiple traumatic injuries and disorders
09	Other traumatic injuries and disorders
41	Symptoms

Table B.12
Data Underlying Figure 4.12—Cause of Injury for EMS Line-of-Duty
Fatalities, 1998–2001

Cause	Fatalities					
	1998	**1999**	**2000**	**2001**	**Total**	**Percent**
Aircraft accident	9	10	6	1	26	57
Motor vehicle accident	5	2	2	3	12	26
Heart attack/stress	1			2	3	7
Struck by vehicle		2			2	4
Drowning	1				1	2
Illness				1	1	2
Homicide					0	0
Other				1	1	2
Total	16	14	8	8	46	100

SOURCE: RAND tabulation of National EMS Memorial Service (2002), excluding those EMS responders (total of 6 fatalities) covered by the U.S. Fire Administration Firefighter Fatality Database.
NOTE: Total percentages may not add due to rounding.